the booze book

the booze book

the joy of drink

Stories, poems, ballads, reflections, epigrams,
sketches, quizzes, cartoons, entertainments,
paintings, and inspirations about the
glory of the grape.

edited by ralph schoenstein

P⚹P

a playboy press book

For Eve-Lynn
But I get a kick out of you

Published simultaneously in the United States and Canada by Playboy Press, Chicago, Illinois. Printed in the United States of America. Library of Congress Catalog Card Number: 73-91654. ISBN #87223-394-4. First edition.

PLAYBOY and Rabbit Head design are trademarks of Playboy, 919 North Michigan Avenue, Chicago, Illinois 60611 (U.S.A.), Reg. U.S. Pat. Off., marca registrada, marque déposée.

DESIGNED BY JACK JAGET

acknowledgments

"Why We Should Drink" by Kingsley Amis from *On Drink* by Kingsley Amis. Copyright © 1970, 1972 by Kingsley Amis and *The Daily Telegraph.* Reprinted by permission of Harcourt Brace Jovanovich, Inc.

"Port Wine—A Perfect Reason to Leave the Ladies" by Alec Waugh from *Signature* magazine. Copyright © 1973 by Diners' Club. Reprinted by permission of Brandt and Brandt.

"What's Your Alcoholic IQ?" originally titled *A Drink Quiz* by Joseph C. Stacey from PLAYBOY magazine. Copyright © 1954 by Joseph C. Stacey.

"If Grant Had Been Drinking at Appomattox" by James Thurber. Copyright © 1945 by James Thurber. Copyright © 1973 by Helen W. Thurber and Rosemary Thurber Sauers. From *The Thurber Carnival* published by Harper & Row, Publishers, New York. Originally printed in *The New Yorker* magazine.

"The Social Status of the Martini" by James Villas from *Esquire* magazine. Reprinted by permission of *Esquire* magazine. Copyright © 1973 by Esquire, Inc.

"There Is a Tavern in the Town" by Frederic Birmingham from *Falstaff's Complete Beer Book* published by Universal-Award House, Inc. Copyright © 1973 by Frederic Birmingham. Reprinted by permission of the author.

"Name Your Poison" by Ray Russel from PLAYBOY magazine. Copyright © by Ray Russell. Reprinted by permission of the author.

"The Old House at Home" by Joseph Mitchell from *McSorley's Wonderful Saloon* published by Duell, Sloan and Pearce. Copyright © 1940 by Joseph Mitchell. Copyright renewed. Reprinted by permission of Harold Ober Associates, Incorporated.

"Cocktail Hour" by Robert Benchley from *Benchley—Or Else!* by Robert Benchley. Copyright © 1932, 1936, 1938 by Robert C. Benchley. Reprinted by permission of Harper & Row, Publishers.

contents

 # introduction

IF MASTERS and Johnson can point the way to one kind of fun, then Samuel Johnson can point out another, man's second favorite indoor recreation.

"There is nothing which has yet been contrived by man," Sam said, "by which so much happiness is produced as by a good tavern or inn."

This book, of course, is hardly a substitute for the kind of evening that the good doctor enjoyed in an inn. Reading about drinking is roughly similar to looking at slides of intercourse. But if you happen to be doing some quiet imbibing at home, then a blend of the word and the grape can heighten your happiness. Pour yourself a glass of Château Mouton-Rothschild '29 or even some Boone's Farm Apple Wine and enjoy what Benjamin Franklin, Kingsley Amis, William Shakespeare, Ogden Nash, W. C. Fields, and the Israelites have had to say about drink. Enjoy some quizzes, epigrams, cartoons, anecdotes and even a horoscope about the pastime that moved Alec Waugh to say, "Human beings are at their best in bars."

In putting together *The Booze Book,* I wandered from the Bible to the *Guinness Book of World Records,* from ancient Rome to Robert Benchley, skimming off enlightenment, inspiration and fun for you to dip into whenever you can steal a few minutes from the world that is too much with us. And that's how this book is to be read: not forward, backward, or any other predetermined way, but dipped into from time to time, like a champagne punch on a summer day.

Like all anthologies, this one reflects the taste of the anthologist; and in matters of taste, as the Romans said, argument makes no sense. You may very well feel that your uncle knows more about martinis than Frederic Birmingham, James Villas or W. C. Fields, that you've been to 19 bars that were wilder than the one that Mencken writes about, and that your platoon sergeant knew some toasts that William Iversen never heard. But I'll bet he didn't know the longest distance that a champagne cork ever flew from an unheated bottle, a bit of scholarship you'll find in here, not far from a poem by Byron, instructions for starting a wine cellar, and some bawdy tales of the greatest Western saloons. It's all a matter of taste, as the boys in McSorley's used to say when they warmed their ale on a stove. Nevertheless, I am certain that the words and drawings to follow will give you some degree of pleasure as they illuminate an activity that has been with us since the world's first drinker, about whom the Bible says, "And Noah drank of the wine and was drunken."

Of course, if *you* had to go on a cruise with two camels, two cobras, two aardvarks and two giraffes, you'd take a little something yourself.

RALPH SCHOENSTEIN

The same child who once asked why the sky is blue grew up to ask why people drink. Kingsley Amis, a complete imbiber, here presents a thoughtful reply.

why we should drink

by kingsley amis

ANTHROPOLOGISTS assure us that wherever we find man he speaks. Chimpanzee-lovers notwithstanding, no animal other than man is capable of laughter. And, although some undiscovered tribe in the Brazilian jungle might conceivably prove an exception tomorrow, every present-day society uses alcohol, as have the majority of those of the past. I am not denying that we share other important pleasures with the brute creation, merely stating the basic fact that conversation, hilarity and drink are connected in a profoundly human, peculiarly intimate way.

There is a choice of conclusions from this. One would be that no such healthy linkage exists in the case of other drugs: a major reason for being on guard against them. More to the point, the collective social benefits of drinking altogether (on this evidence) outweigh the individual disasters it may precipitate. A team of American investigators concluded recently that, without the underpinning provided by alcohol and the relaxation it affords, Western society would have collapsed irretrievably at about the time of the First World War. Not only is drink here to stay; the moral seems to be that when it goes, we go too.

It has certainly increased its hold on our lives with the world-wide move to the towns and the general increase in prosperity. Wine and beer are—in origin, in the countries that produce them—drinks of the village and the poorer classes; gin and whiskey belong to the city and, these days at any rate, the rather better off. In other words, our drinks are getting stronger as well as more numerous.

The strains and stresses of urban living, to coin a phrase, are usually held accountable for these increases. I should not dissent from this exactly, but I should single out one stress (or strain) as distinctly more burdensome, and also more widespread, than most: sudden confrontation with complete or comparative strangers in circumstances requiring a show of relaxation and amiability—an experience that I, for one, never look forward to without misgiving, even though I nearly always turn out to enjoy it in the event. While the village remained the social unit, strangers appeared seldom, and when they did were heavily outnumbered by your family, your friends, people you had known all your life. Nowadays, in the era of the business lunch, the dinner party, the office party, the anything-and-everything party, strangers pour over the horizon all the time.

The reason why I, and most others, usually turn out to enjoy meeting such creatures is simply and obviously the co-presence of drink. The human race has not devised any way of dissolving barriers, getting to know the other chap fast, breaking the ice, that is one-tenth as handy and efficient as letting you and the other chap, or chaps, cease to be totally sober at about the same rate in agreeable surroundings. Well and good, the serious student of the effects of drink will retort in the grim, curmudgeongly tone peculiar to serious students of the effects of drink; well and good, but what about what

Here's to the maiden of bashful fifteen;
Here's to the widow of fifty;
Here's to the flaunting, extravagant queen,
And here's to the housewife that's thrifty!
Let the toast pass;
Drink to the lass;
I'll warrant she'll prove an excuse for the glass.

—RICHARD BRINSLEY SHERIDAN (1757–1816)

happens later? What about those who drink, not to cease to be totally sober, but to get drunk? What about the man who drinks *on his own*?

Well, what about it and them and him? I have nothing to offer, nothing more to add to serious sociological speculation about the whys and wherefores of indulgence in alcohol. Or only this: leaving aside dipsomaniacs, most or many of whom are born, not made, I feel that there is very little we can safely add, in discussing our motives for drinking, to the verdict of the poet who said we do it because we are dry, "or lest we should be by-and-by, or any other reason why."

wine and water

by g.k. chesterton

OLD NOAH he had an ostrich farm and fowls on the largest
  scale,
He ate his egg with a ladle in an egg-cup big as a pail,
And the soup he took was Elephant Soup, and the fish he
  took was Whale,
But they all were small to the cellar he took when he set out
  to sail.
And Noah he often said to his wife when he sat down to
  dine,
"I don't care where the water goes if it doesn't get into the
  wine."

The cataract of the cliff of heaven fell blinding off the brink
As if it would wash the stars away as suds go down a sink;
The seven heavens came roaring down for the throats of hell
  to drink,
And Noah he cocked his eye and said, "It looks like rain, I
  think.
The water has drowned the Matterhorn as deep as a Mendip
  mine,
But I don't care where the water goes if it doesn't get into the
  wine."

But Noah he sinned, and we have sinned; on tipsy feet we
  trod,

"I'm a hooker—that's *what a nice girl like me*
is doing in a place like this."

Till a great big black teetotaller was sent to us for a rod,
And you can't get wine at a P.S.A., or chapel, or Eisteddfod,
For the Curse of Water has come again because of the wrath
    of God;
And water is on the Bishop's board and the Higher Thinker's
    shrine,
But I don't care where the water goes if it doesn't get into the
    wine.

You will never read a more literate and fervent essay on the pleasures of drink than this one by Alec Waugh. He has spent a lifetime loving port, but a wino he's not.

port wine –
a perfect reason to
leave the ladies

by alec waugh

IN THESE my declining years I have made Tangier my base. My friends in London say, "Surely there must be something that you miss there." If they expect me to answer, "Watching cricket on color TV," I surprise them. "I miss vintage port," I say. For over 50 years it has been my solace and support. It is rich, smooth, fragrant, velvety. It rounds off perfectly a lunch or dinner. It is a wine to be sipped slowly, accompanied by a dry biscuit, cake, cheese, fruits or walnuts. When thirst and hunger are assuaged, it maintains and embellishes the glow engendered by good food and wine in congenial company. It is a wine to be sat over for 20, 40 minutes, for an hour, after "the ladies have left the gentlemen to their port," with the decanter passing clockwise round the table. For me, no meal can be perfect that is not rounded off by vintage port, and when in the spring of 1935 I became for the first time the proprietor of a cellar, my first act was to fill one of the bins with bottle of it.

The house, a Queen Anne rectory, had been built appropriately in 1703. Appropriately because that was the year of the Methuen Treaty, which reduced the import duty on Portuguese wines to £7 a tun (the 252-gallon cask in which bulk wine is shipped), while French and German wines were taxed at the rate of £55 a tun. The treaty was one of the House of Orange's many acts of reprisal against Catholic France in general and Louis XIV in particular, and it was a first chapter in the romantic saga of vintage port.

That saga is the most dramatic in the whole history of wine. The purpose of Queen Anne's ministers had been to make the English drink Portuguese table wines instead of French and German. But

"Oh, just whatever you can pronounce, Fred."

nothing turned out as planned. There is an old proverb that you can
take a horse to the water, but you cannot make it drink. The English,
who had owned Aquitaine for 200 years and had acquired a taste for
the full-bodied wines of Bordeaux, found the wines from Lisbon and
Oporto thin and flavorless. To make them palatable, they softened
them with treacle, deepened the color with elderberries, laced them
with brandy, and then warmed them up. This concoction was known
as Negur, after a distinguished colonel who served under Marl-
borough. It was this fiery brew that Boswell and Dr. Johnson drank.
They consumed at least a bottle each night, usually dividing another
bottle after that. When Boswell complained of the bad effects this
heavy drinking was having on him, a friend assured him that it was
better to be palsied in youth than not keep company with such a man
as Johnson. Those were the days when most dinner parties ended

with the men under the table and young servants on their knees loosening the diners' cravats. Raymond Postgate wrote, "Our ancestors who spent whole days fox hunting were three-bottle men no doubt, but we don't live their lives; also they died young, purple or yellow, gouty, savage-tempered and inflamed; the memoirs of the eighteenth century are full of the results of port drinking." But the port they drank was very different from the wine that the Victorians drank and that we drink today.

Real port didn't come on the scene until wine-makers realized the potential of vineyards that lie much higher up the Douro River, in a rugged terrain of rocks and gorges, of torrents and precipices, where the vines are planted on artfully built terraces, walled so that the rains will not wash away the soil, a peculiar clay alternating with granite. The summers there are very hot. The winters are very cold. And the grapes are so full of sugar that the fermentation has to be checked with a heavy dose of alcohol. My brother Evelyn in *Brideshead Revisited*, looking back tolerantly on the sins of youth, compared the juvenile vices of his Oxford with "the spirits they mix with the pure grape of the Douro, heady stuff full of dark ingredients that at once enriched and retarded the whole process of adolescence as the spirit checks the fermentation of the wine, renders it undrinkable so that it must lie in the dark, year in, year out, until it is brought up at last fit for the table."

The wine from the Douro can be matured either in bottle or in cask, and herein lies a pertinent part of the romance of port. At the very time the possibilities of the wines from the upper Douro were being recognized someone invented the bottle that could lie on its side, with the cork in contact with the liquid so that the cork would not grow dry and shrink. It is hard for us who take for granted the bottle that can be safely binned to realize that it was not until 1780 that such a bottle appeared. Up till then bottles were squat and short-necked and broad in the beam so that they could stand upon the table.

Only a small percentage of the wine that is brought from the upper Douro to Oporto is converted into vintage port. In exceptionally good years the shippers declare a vintage, and in those years only a portion—the best portion of the wine—is given a special treatment. The wine destined for this honor is kept in Oporto for 18 months before bottling. The corks are branded with the date and the shipper's name; the cork is waxed, and a splash of white paint is placed on the foot—the punt—of the bottle to show which side up it should lie. It then waits in cellars for 10, 20, 40 years. Vintage port is an English drink, invented by Englishmen, to suit the vagaries of our climate and our way of life. It is the wine for rectories and colleges, for clubs and country houses. It is too heavy for southern Europe and is not alcoholic enough for Scandinavians. It is a protection against damp and chill rather than snow and frost.

The ports that I laid down in 1935 were for immediate drinking, as soon as they had rested—Croft's 1912, Graham's 1920, Sea Vista 1923—a year for which Oyley was one of the few shippers to declare a vintage. When I had finished those, I planned to go on to Dow's 1924. For the '40's, taking a long view, I bought 10 cases of Cockburn's 1927; at that time you could buy the '27 vintage for £3 a dozen.

With proud and reverent eyes I watched my wine merchant's cellar men arrange the bottles, separating the rows with thin strips of wood. I had done everything to assure that the bottles would keep in prime condition. I covered with asbestos the hot-water pipe that ran under the roof, so that the cellar temperature would not run too high. I wondered how soon I should be able to broach the '27.

I did not think it would be ready before 1939. In October 1938, at the time of Munich—when the air was full of omen—I broached a bottle, "just to see." It was good, but it was not ready, and in June 1940 when the house was closed—I was in the army and my wife was taking the children to Australia—I resisted the temptation to open a bottle my last night at home. "One has to believe in something," I told myself. "I must believe that one day the war'll be won and I'll be returning to that cellar." Luckily I did return. The house was mercifully taken over not by an army mess but by a *crèche*-load of

---

Getting There Was All the Fun   "A woman drove me to drink," W. C. Fields once said, "and I never even wrote to thank her."

---

evacuated children. Infants of five and six can and did inflict considerable damage up to a height of four foot six, but they do not pillage cellars. In September 1946 I found my Cockburn '27 rounded and mature.

The happiest of the many happy hours I spent in that cellar were devoted to the care of port. When my elder son and daughter were five and four years old, I took them down to watch me decant port for the weekend guests. I wanted them from the start to think of wine in terms of ritual. I would move the bottle from the bin in a wicker basket with the greatest care, so as not to disturb the sediment and the crust which had formed inside the bottle. On the cellar table would be a decanter into the mouth of which had been fitted a strip of muslin, held in place by a silver filter. There were beside it a corkscrew and a lighted candle. With the handle of the corkscrew I would chip away the wax that protected the cork. Then I would insert the point of the screw; once in four times the cork would break or crumble. The children at my side would say, "I hope the cork doesn't break," but they said it in the secret hope it would. Everything was more dramatic when it did. They enjoyed seeing me cut away at the cork and force it back into the bottle. Alternatively I

The Roar of Relief Awakening one morning after a titanic Night Before, W. C. Fields heard the fizzing noise of an Alka-Seltzer being dissolved in a glass of water.
"Can't anyone," he cried, "do something about that racket?"

---

would give the flange of the bottle a sharp tap with the back of a heavy carving knife. If the blow is correctly timed, the flange will fly off, encircling the cork with a clean ring of glass. But usually I preferred to cut the cork, a method that could be unsatisfactory because with some part of the cork remaining in the narrow neck, the wine at first comes in a trickle; then that piece of cork slides back into the bottle, wine gushes out, and some of the precious liquid may be lost.

Before the wine is poured, the mouth of the bottle has to be wiped with a clean cloth. No trouble is too great to take with vintage port. The bottle has to be tipped very slowly. By means of the lighted candle placed beneath, you can tell when the line of sediment and broken crust reaches the neck of the bottle; then you must stop pouring. Meredith has said, "Old wine denies us the full bottle," and this is truer of vintage port than of burgundy and claret; the dregs are usually half-an-inch high. They can be employed profitably in the kitchen as an ingredient in sauces or dressings.

It was a happy day for me when, 25 years later, I initiated my eldest grandson into the ritual. The cook's name was Mrs. Merchant, and my grandson would walk up the cellar steps carrying the decanted bottle—still with its dregs—proudly chanting, "Dirty wine for Mrs. Merch." He will always remember this, I thought.

Vintage port stands alone, in a class apart from other wines. When Victorian and Edwardian squires laid down a pipe (672 bottles) for their heir's christening, it was with vintage port that they lined the bins. But that does not mean that the upper reaches of the Douro do

"I'd like you to meet the rage of Paris."

not produce other types of wine that are by any standard excellent. There are, for instance, the wines that are variously known as "crusted," "late bottled," or "vintage character." Blended wines of different years that are bottled after four or five years in wood throw a crust and after six years or so can make a respectable appearance on the table. They have no guarantee of provenance; you have to trust your shipper and your wine merchant—and, where port is concerned, you almost always can.

There are also wines from Portugal that mature in wood. And there are "port-type" wines that have their origin in many other parts of the world. But one can take satisfaction in knowing that in the United States and Great Britain no wine can be labeled port that does not come from the prescribed area of the upper Douro. Port-type wines from other areas have to be labeled Californian, Australian or South African.

The wines that mature in wood in Oporto include the white port that can be taken instead of a dry sherry but is preferable as a long drink with ice and soda water. It can be very refreshing after a morning on the golf course. There is the light, reddish wine that the French take as an aperitif. There is the rather rough wine that you are served in English pubs when you ask for a port and lemon. This is often called ruby port, but it is not genuine ruby until it has been eight years in cask, by which time it achieves a full ruby color. Another four years in wood and the color changes, becoming tawny. Tawny port does not improve in bottle, and should be drunk within six months. It is a noble wine.

There is plenty of excellent ruby and tawny port in the United States. The production of it demands incessant and expert care. There is evaporation in the cask, and the evaporated liquid has to be replenished with fresh wine and renewed with brandy. Shippers have to maintain a constant homogeniety of taste and color for their different brands; Harveys Hunting Port must always look and taste the same.

It is not surprising that the best tawny should be expensive. But it is worth the price, and it can be obtained without too much difficulty in Tangier. I relish it but I miss vintage port. That is unique. May I beg my readers to take every opportunity of sampling it next time they are in England. It can be obtained by the glass in most good restaurants. And may I suggest that they ask the wine waiter which year's vintage they are being served. They will find it interesting to compare years. The wines will be different. But of one thing they can be certain: each vintage port in its own way will be supreme.

What's your alcoholic IQ? No, that doesn't mean Intake in Quarts. It just means take this little quiz and then see the bottom of page 17 for the answers.

what's your alcoholic iq?

THE MAN who drinks spirituous liquors merely to get swacked will guzzle the stuff indiscriminately from shaving mugs or flower pots. But the man of taste, the man who appreciates the better brews and blends—this man recognizes a drink for what it is: a symbol of gracious living. Such a man is aware of the importance of sipping the right drink from the right glass. He knows the hazards of drinking champagne from an open-toed slipper, and he knows a good deal more besides. He would, with minimum pondering, match the glasses on this page with their proper drinks, making the top score of ten. Can you? Eight is also an excellent score, and six is not too bad. But any lower than that and we'll send you back to the shaving mugs and flower pots.

a—OLD FASHIONED   f—COCKTAIL

b—SHERRY   g—WHISKEY

c—PILSENER   h—HIGHBALL

d—CHAMPAGNE   i—CORDIAL OR LIQUEUR

e—BRANDY   j—WINE

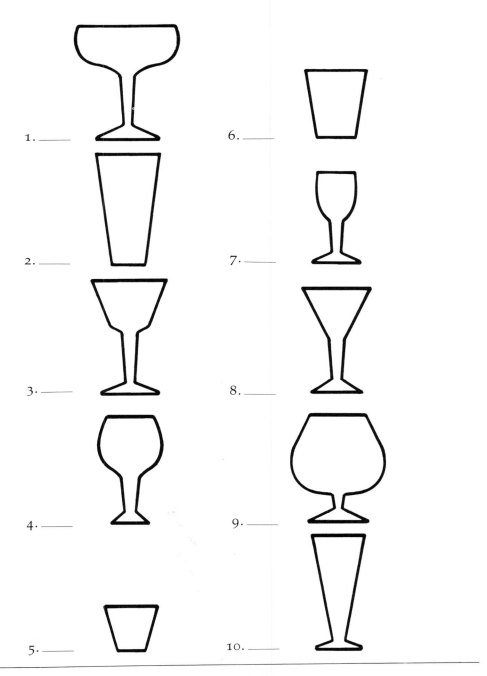

1. _____

2. _____

3. _____

4. _____

5. _____

6. _____

7. _____

8. _____

9. _____

10. _____

cast away care

by thomas dekker

(1570?–1641?)

CAST away care; he that loves sorrow
    Lengthens not a day, nor can buy to-morrow;
    Money is trash; and he that will spend it,
Let him drink merrily, Fortune will send it.
    Merrily, merrily, merrily, oh, ho!
    Play it off stiffly, we may not part so.

Wine is a charm, it heats the blood too,
Cowards it will harm, if the wine be good too;
Quickens the wit, and makes the back able;
Scorn to submit to the watch or constable.
    Merrily, merrily, etc.

Pots fly about, give us more liquor,
Brothers of a rout, our brains will flow quicker;
Empty the cask; score it up we care not,
Fill up the pots again, and drink on and spare not.
    Merrily, merrily, etc.

Drunkenness itself has never seemed inherently funny to me. Nevertheless, this particular story about that condition is a comic gem, my favorite Civil War tale.

if grant
had been drinking
at appomattox

by james thurber

THE MORNING of the ninth of April, 1865, dawned beautifully. General Meade was up with the first streaks of crimson in the eastern sky. General Hooker and General Burnside were up, and had breakfasted, by a quarter after eight. The day continued beautiful. It drew on toward eleven o'clock. General Ulysses S. Grant was still not up. He was asleep in his famous old navy hammock, swung high above the floor of his headquarters' bedroom. Headquarters was distressingly disarranged: papers were strewn on the floor; confidential notes from spies scurried here and there in the breeze from an open window; the dregs of an overturned bottle of wine flowed pinkly across an important military map.

Corporal Shultz, of the Sixty-fifth Ohio Volunteer Infantry, aide to General Grant, came into the outer room, looked around him, and sighed. He entered the bedroom and shook the General's hammock roughly. General Ulysses S. Grant opened one eye.

"Pardon, sir," said Corporal Shultz, "but this is the day of surrender. You ought to be up, sir."

"Don't swing me," said Grant, sharply, for his aide was making the hammock sway gently. "I feel terrible," he added, and he turned over and closed his eye again.

"General Lee will be here any minute now," said the Corporal firmly, swinging the hammock again.

"Will you cut that out?" roared Grant. "D'ya want to make me sick, or what?" Shultz clicked his heels and saluted. "What's he coming here for?" asked the General.

"This is the day of surrender, sir," said Shultz. Grant grunted bitterly.

"Three hundred and fifty generals in the Northern armies," said Grant, "and he has to come to *me* about this. What time is it?"

"You're the Commander-in-Chief, that's why," said Corporal Shultz. "It's eleven twenty-five, sir."

"Don't be crazy," said Grant. "Lincoln is the Commander-in-Chief. Nobody in the history of the world ever surrendered before lunch. Doesn't he know that an army surrenders on its stomach?" He pulled a blanket up over his head and settled himself again.

"The generals of the Confederacy will be here any minute now," said the Corporal. "You really ought to be up, sir."

Grant stretched his arms above his head and yawned.

"All right, all right," he said. He rose to a sitting position and stared about the room. "This place looks awful," he growled.

"You must have had quite a time of it last night, sir," ventured Shultz.

"Yeh," said General Grant, looking around for his clothes, "I was wrassling some general. Some general with a beard."

Shultz helped the commander of the Northern armies in the field to find his clothes.

"Where's my other sock?" demanded Grant. Shultz began to look around for it. The General walked uncertainly to a table and poured a drink from a bottle.

"I don't think it wise to drink, sir," said Shultz.

"Nev' mind about me," said Grant, helping himself to a second, "I can take it or let it alone. Didn' ya ever hear the story about the fella

Travelers' Aid   "Always carry a flagon of whiskey in case of snakebite," said W. C. Fields, "and furthermore always carry a small snake."

went to Lincoln to complain about me drinking too much? 'So-and-So says Grant drinks too much,' this fella said. 'So-and-So is a fool,' said Lincoln. So this fella went to What's-His-Name and told him what Lincoln said and he came roarin' to Lincoln about it. 'Did you tell So-and-So I was a fool?' he said. 'No,' said Lincoln, 'I thought he knew it.'" The General smiled, reminiscently, and had another drink. "*That's* how I stand with Lincoln," he said, proudly.

The soft thudding sound of horses' hooves came through the open window. Shultz hurriedly walked over and looked out.

"Know why this marriage is gonna last, Flo?
Becaush we gotta lot in common."

"Hoof steps," said Grant, with a curious chortle.

"It is General Lee and his staff," said Shultz.

"Show him in," said the General, taking another drink. "And see what the boys in the back room will have."

Shultz walked smartly over to the door, opened it, saluted, and stood aside. General Lee, dignified against the blue of the April sky, magnificent in his dress uniform, stood for a moment framed in the

The praise of Bacchus then the sweet musician sung,
Of Bacchus ever fair and ever young:
The jolly god in triumph comes;
Sound the trumpets; beat the drums;
Flushed with a purple grace
He shows his honest face:
Now give the hautboys breath; he comes, he comes.

Bacchus ever fair and young
Drinking joys did first ordain;
Bacchus' blessings are a treasure;
Drinking is the soldier's pleasure;
Rich the treasure;
Sweet the pleasure;
Sweet is pleasure after pain.

—JOHN DRYDEN (1631–1700)

doorway. He walked in, followed by his staff. They bowed, and stood silent. General Grant stared at them. He only had one boot on and his jacket was unbuttoned.

"I know who you are," said Grant. "You're Robert Browning, the poet."

"This is General Robert E. Lee," said one of his staff, coldly.

"Oh," said Grant. "I thought he was Robert Browning. He certainly looks like Robert Browning. There was a poet for you, Lee: Browning. Did ja ever read 'How They Brought the Good News from Ghent to Aix'? 'Up Derek, to saddle, up Derek, away; up Dunder, up Blitzen, up Prancer, up Dancer, up Bouncer, up Vixen, up—'"

"Shall we proceed at once to the matter in hand?" asked General Lee, his eyes disdainfully taking in the disordered room.

"Some of the boys was wrassling here last night," explained Grant. "I threw Sherman, or some general a whole lot like Sherman. It was pretty dark." He handed a bottle of Scotch to the commanding officer of the Southern armies, who stood holding it, in amazement and discomfiture. "Get a glass, somebody," said Grant, looking straight at General Longstreet. "Didn't I meet you at Cold Harbor?" he asked. General Longstreet did not answer.

"I should like to have this over with as soon as possible," said Lee. Grant looked vaguely at Shultz, who walked up close to him, frowning.

"The surrender, sir, the surrender," said Corporal Shultz in a whisper.

"Oh sure, sure," said Grant. He took another drink. "All right," he said. "Here we go." Slowly, sadly, he unbuckled his sword. Then he handed it to the astonished Lee. "There you are, General," said Grant. "We dam' near licked you. If I'd been feeling better we *would* of licked you."

Not to be outdone by Alec Waugh's rhapsody to port, James Villas here sings the praises of what has replaced baseball as the Great American Pastime: drinking martinis.

How far ahead of his time was that potted pioneer, W. C. Fields!

the social status
of the martini

by james villas

WHILE there can be no doubt that pinstripe suits and four-door sedans and plastic credit cards have never won the overwhelming approval of the present younger generation, no symbol of middle-class corruption stands out so blatantly or provokes more wrath in our junior citizens than the all-American Martini. An incurable and not so old Martini-fancier myself who also happens to enjoy part-time college teaching, I've been in key positions over the past decade to witness this age group's brutal attack on the country's most classic cocktail. Back in the Sixties, when grass was taking root, the onslaught was predictably sluggish. Then, almost overnight, the term "Martini" became generic for any strong alcoholic drink, and suffice it to say that today if I had to depend on those wonderfully exciting individuals below the age of twenty-five as drinking partners, I'd be hopelessly parched in a matter of days!

What does the Martini represent to the youngsters? I asked my students and they answered with vehemence. Generally, the Martini signifies absolute decadence. Specifically, it means a bitter, medicinal-tasting beverage. It stands for everything from phony bourgeois values and social snobbery to jaded alcoholism and latent masochism. No matter where you inquire throughout the country, the response, with no exaggeration, is one-hundred percent the same: young people do not like Martinis and they're not drinking them. Ever! Anywhere! Not in bars, not in restaurants, not on airplanes, and certainly not at home. Many have never even tasted one and quite possibly never will. (If they indulge at all, their

"Now that y'mention it, ma'am, I could stand *a little action.
Got any good gay bars around here?*"

preference is white wine on the rocks, an occasional beer, or pitchers of Sangria-like glop.)

Well, the hell with them. Which brings me to the good tidings: the opinions and drinking habits of the post-Korean generation have had *absolutely no recognizable influence* on the social status of our noble potion. For once, the fortifications on this side of the generation gap have held firm. In fact, the Martini, in one form or another, not only continues to reign supreme among cocktails but is actually gaining in popularity each year with the over-thirty bunch of the middle and upper classes.

As any bartender in any major American bar or restaurant will verify, the Martini now outsells all other alcoholic drinks two to one. Simply out of curiosity, I recently perched myself for a marathon

---

The Smoothest Eraser   "I drink," said Jackie Gleason, "to remove warts and pimples from the people I'm looking at."

---

two-hour sit-down at the famous Oak Room Bar at The Plaza Hotel in New York to observe my faithful bartenders, Teddy Warias and Mike Scrippens, mixing drinks. During that period of time, they received orders for approximately five hundred cocktails, nearly three hundred of which were Martinis. Teddy minced no words of explanation:

"Face it," he insisted, "with today's frantic pace of life and frustrations, people—women as well as men—are not only drinking more but they want the fastest pickup possible, and nothing solves the problem better than a few Martinis. Customers here average between two and three before lunch, and they all order them extra dry. Why? Generally to get loaded!"

Another favorite bartender in New York, Vincent at the Polo Lounge of The Westbury Hotel, verified in even more enlightening terms everything Teddy had said.

"There's no doubt about it, the Martini is more popular than ever before here, and it's because by midday or late afternoon, drinkers —regulars and out-of-towners alike—want something strong to either get them through the day or relax them in the evening. People used to all settle for a Bloody Mary or Screwdriver to revive the spirits, but in the past few years they've been looking for the distinct kick of a Martini."

Even at youth-supported citadels in New York like Friday's and Maxwell's Plum, where hundreds of rosy cheeks eschew the Silver

Bullet in favor of more respectable libations, plenty of the hard stuff is still blended with vermouth to satisfy the decadent, well-heeled, foreign sinners over thirty. By phone from Los Angeles and Kansas City: the same guilty verdict. In airplanes: miniature bottles in plastic racks full of so-and-so company's Martinis selling like hot cakes at a buck and a half. At the homes of friends: every ingredient imaginable for the making of a Martini. After a few weeks of talking and watching and, to be sure, further endangering my own liver, any suspicions I might originally have had (via my students) over the drink's popularity were gradually dispelled.

Although the Martini per se is still at the top of the social register, I am a little shocked at the degree to which the cocktail's components, preparation, and garnishments have been modified or changed during the last decade. For semi-purists like myself, a Martini has always implied one thing and one thing only: good, aromatic gin with a suggestion of dry vermouth served very cold with a twist of lemon. Except for the fact that I now prefer my drink on the rocks instead of straight up, my taste has never changed. As far as I am personally concerned, any mixture not comprising the distinct flavors of juniper, dry vermouth, and lemon is simply not a Martini but some alien concoction. Curiously enough, I know now I'm part of a small minority.

The most radical change in the Martini of recent years is the overwhelming victory of vodka over gin. Unlike in the past, when ordering a Martini meant automatically a gin Martini, today you must specify which spirit you prefer. Throughout the country, bartenders and aficionados will tell you that vodka is outselling gin three to one. Why? For many reasons. First, advertising or something or somebody has managed to convince drinkers that vodka has no odor. As a result, some people believe they can down six ounces of vodka at lunch, return to work, and have the breath of an angel. (As for the scent of the vermouth, well, who gives it a thought?) Second, the mild taste of vodka challenges the robust flavor of even the finest imported gin, encouraging those who might not normally order a Martini to enjoy a rather bland but sturdy jolt. Third is the ridiculous myth that vodka does not bring on a hangover. Bull! Too much of any alcoholic beverage that is loaded with arcane botanicals guarantees what the French so appropriately term "une gueule de bois" (a wooden mouth), and particularly when you play dangerous games with Martinis made with 100-proof vodka (94 proof is the absolute maximum for gin), you'd be wise to check your stock of bromides and aspirin.

Another trend quickly developing in the world of the Martini is

"I don't give a damn—it still *needs nutmeg!*"

drinking the cocktail on the rocks. Twenty years ago the idea would have been outlandish. Orthodox purists still argue convincingly that the only proper way to savor an ice-cold Martini is straight up, and most distinguished bars still keep a few frosted stemmed glasses in the coolor for this type of customer. However, it's been a long while since I've noticed anyone in the kitchen practicing the old tradition of placing a pitcher of Martinis in the refrigerator or slipping a few pieces of delicate stemware between the frozen foods. There's no doubt that adding ice to a Martini gradually dilutes the spirits and,

If all be true that I do think,
There are five reasons we should drink:
Good wine—a friend—or being dry—
Or lest we should be by-and-by—
Or any other reason why.

—HENRY ALDRICH (1647–1710)

unless consumed rapidly, makes those last few sips disgusting in taste. On the other hand, nothing is more equally offensive than the warm dregs of a straight-up Martini. Since I insist that my gin and vermouth remain well chilled, I've opted for the new method but usually take great care to remove the ice about midway through the drink, thus assuring minimum dilution.

Whether a Martini is enjoyed straight up or on the rocks, drinkers throughout the country do agree that the cocktail must be blended in a separate container and absolutely never in the glass from which it is imbibed. If it is prepared correctly, a little vermouth is first poured into a large mixing glass, then the gin or vodka, then the ice. Once the mélange has been sufficiently chilled, it is either poured into a frosted Martini glass or over fresh ice in a larger but shorter glass. As for the old notion of bruising the gin (and I suppose vodka also) while stirring Martinis, well, that's still another myth which is fortunately being dispelled during the present hedonistic age. Just recently, people standing at the King Cole Bar in New York's St. Regis Hotel gasped as they watched Jimmy, the veteran bartender, attacking my Martini as if the long spoon were an air drill directed against concrete. The concoction was sublime.

I do detect a serious problem regarding certain alien ingredients that are often added to Martinis as additives to or substitutes for dry vermouth. It appears that in some places the most jaded Martini drinkers, bored with the same flavor, are adding drops of such spirits as sherry, Scotch, and absurdly enough, even brandy. Elsewhere I understand that a British cocktail called a Pink Gin (made with Angostura bitters) is attracting a few infidels. And from the Beverly Wilshire Hotel in Los Angeles, the charming director of guest relations, Helen Chaplin, informs me that the popular "Sunny Special" in El Padrino Bar is vodka or gin, served in a glass mug with a splash of water and a Martini garnish. Sacrilege!

No less serious is the intrusion in the sacred Martini glass of obscene garnishments. A staunch advocator of the innocent and sensible lemon twist, I have never understood how a serious Martini fancier could destroy the drink's sensual flavor by plopping in a salty pimiento-olive or one of those rancid miniature cocktail onions (which immediately transforms a Martini into a Gibson). Yet, these traditional garnishments are mild compared to other base objects creeping into the cocktail. In the South I've seen someone drop a maraschino cherry in a fine imported gin Martini. In the Midwest it's not rare to find in Martinis olives stuffed with onions, hazelnuts, filbert nuts, and, most nauseating of all, anchovies. And on the West Coast the most fashionable garnishment for our delicate libation is a mammoth green olive with an ultra-chic wooden toothpick jabbed through the middle. At this rate I wouldn't be surprised one day to see capers, parsley, peanuts, and God knows what other brilliant adornments floating around inside the glass!

So, as the uninitiated can surmise, we who are dedicated to the classic Martini and all its wickedness have a few other problems to cope with besides the never-ending futile attempt to establish once and for all the correct proportions of gin (or vodka) and dry vermouth. We may have our differences of opinion, but it's for sure that our mutual enthusiasm, our fidelity, and our total disregard of the opinions of the young have safeguarded the great American cocktail against potential social onslaught. And, of course, the nice thing about the object of our defense is that when such problems get a little out of hand, we always have that evil little aristocrat to console us.

Here's some fermented scholarship by Frederic Birmingham, a fascinating little history of the tavern that expands on the wisdom of Dr. Johnson quoted in my Introduction.

there is a tavern in the town

by frederic birmingham

> *Landlord, fill the flowing bowl,*
> *until it doth run over,*
> *for tonight we'll merry be,*
> *tomorrow we'll be sober.*
>
> 18th CENTURY SONG

THERE'S a touch of true magic in the word tavern. Let's go to a bar?—well, maybe. Let's go to a tavern? You can't say no.

The place is snug, the atmosphere and the decor masculine. The talk is small, but the dreams are big. The bartender's hands are busy, but the hands on the clock momentarily stand still. There is an unspoken fraternity to the place. A man may down his drink with a chuckle or a roar or a sigh, but that's his business and his alone.

Said Dr. Samuel Johnson, who was seldom wrong, and if he were, would find a way of not admitting it:

> There is nothing which has yet been contrived by man, by which so much happiness is produced, as by a good tavern or inn. There is no private house at which people can enjoy themselves so well as in a capital tavern. Let there be ever so great plenty of good things, ever so much grandeur, ever so much elegance, and ever so much desire that everybody should be easy, in the nature of things it cannot be; there must always be some degree of care and anxiety. The master of the house is anxious to entertain his guests, the guests are anxious to be agreeable to him, and no man but a very impudent dog indeed can as freely command what is in another man's house as if it were his own; whereas, at a tavern

there is a general freedom from anxiety. You are sure you are welcome, and the more noise you make, the more trouble you give, the more good things you call for, the welcomer you are. No servant will attend you with the alacrity which waiters do who are incited by the prospect of an immediate reward in proportion as they please.

A relaxed picture indeed.

The aristocracy of ancient Egypt gathered in communal drinking places over 3,000 years ago and asked each other the riddle of the Sphinx or read the morning papyrus over a glass of their Hek. Socrates met with his fellow Greek intellectuals in Athenian taverns to discuss philosophy, although it is an eternal loss to the world that he switched from drinking *pimos* to hemlock.

The Romans and Persians were partial to taverns and set up hostelries along the byways that crisscrossed their empires. The forerunner of the tavern as we know it, however, was an import from the Middle East. During the time of the Crusades some 800 years ago, thousands traveled to and from the Holy Land every year, and it must be confessed that the cultural impact of these pilgrimages was not so much a giving as a taking. The Crusaders, both armed and peaceful, thought of the Saracens as infidels although they could not help but admire their splendid trappings, their works of art, and their seductive women; and the crude Westerners took mental note of much of this and brought it back to imbed into their own culture, which lacked such civilizing sophistries at that time as the Easterners

After gunning his Mercedes the wrong way down a one-way street, the rather inebriated young man was asked where he thought he was going by an inquisitive police officer.
"I'm not really sure," confessed the drunk, "but wherever it is, I must be late, because everybody seems to be coming back already."

had achieved centuries before. The concept of the "inn" was one of the ideas brought back from the East, where conversation and the gentle art of wasting time profitably had long been brought to a point of perfection.

ENGLISH STREETS OF RED LATTICES

The English, being English, set out to improve the Saracen tavern. And it must be confessed that they succeeded. The tavern of

"Sa-a-ay! This looks like a pretty exciting place!"

Elizabethan days, and for about two hundred years thereafter in England, was the source spring of much of her greatness, for it was in taverns that her most illustrious sons chose to gather.

What a place the Falcon Tavern must have been, by the Bankside in London, when Will Shakespeare, rare Ben Jonson, Kit Marlowe (he was killed in a tavern brawl while just a youth, and many thought he could have gone on to outdo the Bard of Avon had he lived). Ford, Beaumont, Fletcher, Drayton and Herrick met there to exchange shafts of wit! They would all sit back and listen, though, when Jonson and Shakespeare crossed words—for those two were the champs. One who was there, Fuller, says it was like the clash of a great Spanish galleon and a British man-of-war. "Master Jonson, like the former, was built far higher in learning: solid but slow in his performances. Shakespeare, like the English man-of-war, lesser in bulk but lighter in sailing, could turn with all tides, talk about and take advantage of all winds by the quickness of his wit and invention." What a stage, that tavern, where the greatest playwright of all time improvised his lines over a glass of ale!

The Mermaid Tavern, over on Bread Street, is far better known today as one of Will's haunts. It was there, according to Beaumont, that the talk ran into the clouds:

> —*What things have we seen*
> *Done at the Mermaid! heard words that have been*
> *So nimble and so full of subtle flame,*
> *As if that everyone from whence they came*
> *Had meant to put his whole wit in a jest,*
> *And had resolved to live a fool the*
> *rest of his dull life. . . .*

Well, I for one believe it. Sir Walter Raleigh, back from buccaneering over the seven seas, established a club at the Mermaid in 1603. Will Shakespeare was a member, of course, and Ben Jonson and the others, and now we add the name of John Donne, the cleric who wrote some of the most passionately erotic poems in the English language. The man who invented the tape-recorder, dammit, was only 350 years too late—think of what Walter and Bill and Ben and John would talk about when their hair was down. Worlds of conquest, worlds of men, worlds of love!

The Boar's Head, near "London stone," was another playground of Will Shakespeare's, and of course he made it immortal by making it the scene of the wild pranks of Prince Hal and "honest Jack Falstaff" in several of his plays. The tavern actually lasted until 1831, when "progress"—as we always seem to term it when we are tearing down some irreplaceable landmark to make way for a shopping center—doomed it to be razed to make way for the approaches of London Bridge. Now the bridge itself is falling down and is being shipped to an American park as a curiosity. Could the Boar's Head have been preserved, we might have been able to purchase from the British not a curiosity, but a shrine. Ah, well.

Such taverns came in time to be recognized by their red lattices. The windows were left open so the drinkers within could peep out and get some fresh air, but lattices and trellises were put up to somewhat shield the customers from prying eyes.

We can see how well the Lord Mayor made out when we read a report made in 1632: "A whole street is in some places but a continuous alehouse, not a shop to be seen between red lattice and red lattice." At about that time, by the way, the innkeeper was known as an "ale draper." I have no way of telling what a female innkeeper was, other than a hostess, but I can tell of the demise of one, Ann Collins, as reported on her epitaph in Gloucestershire:

Twas as she tript from cask to cask,
In at a bung-hole quickly fell,
Suffocation was her task,
She had no time to say farewell.

The political role of the taverns carried over to the British colonies in America, and the whole atmosphere and presence of the tavern is closely interwoven with our Revolutionary period.

The very first American tavern is generally acknowledged to have been The Blue Anchor, obviously a safe haven for seafaring men, which opened its hatches in Philadelphia early in the 1600s.

Sam Adams, often called the father of our Revolution, was himself a brewer, and so was his father before him. The man who became Governor Chittendon of Vermont was originally a brewer. He was among the Green Mountain Boys, led by the Allen brothers, Ethan and Ira, who frequented the Catamount Tavern in Bennington, Vermont. It was Ethan who carried a barrel of beer on his back up Mt. Washington in order to have proper refreshment on hand when he reached the summit. And it was he who threw in the lot of the Green Mountain Boys with the American army after the news came through from Lexington that the British had fired upon colonials in a stand-up confrontation. He later was to capture Fort Ticonderoga for the rebels, and history books have staunchly declared ever since that he pounded on the entrance to the fort with his fist and called upon the commandant to deliver the fort "in the name of the great Jehovah and the Continental Congress." Actually, according to those who were there, the British officer appeared in his nightshirt,

The Beer Drinker.

vastly perturbed at the noise, with his mistress, also in disarray, at his elbow. Because what Ethan had thundered out into the night was: "Come on out of there, you British sons of bitches!" And while the Redcoats might be willing to admit that there were a lot of people who thought of them in that way, they weren't quite sure who *these* guys were.

The U.S. Marine Corps, by tradition filled with legions of Ethan Allen types, had its own beginnings in a tavern, The Tavern of the Tun, in Philadelphia in 1775. Back in New York City, George Washington made his headquarters at Fraunces Tavern, and it still stands there in the heart of the financial district, and a mighty good tavern yet. And in the Indian Queen Tavern, again back in Philly, a man sat, beer in hand (for, like Washington, he loved the brew), poring over a paper he had been writing for some time. At length satisfied, he unknit his brow, smiled, folded up the paper—and then Thomas Jefferson walked out of the tavern with the very first draft of the Declaration of Independence in his pocket.

Such taverns were a wonderfully colorful lot. And they were one of the most important units in the colonial community, as it turned out.

They had humble beginnings. At first the tavern might be no more than a lean-to, put up to accommodate travelers passing through a huddle of cabins nestled in a hacked-out clearing. But then trails turned into primitive roads, boats appeared on the rivers and the towns grew larger; the tavern turned into a cabin and then into something more pretentious. You found them at crossroads, at rope-ferry river crossings such as the one in Bethlehem, Pennsylvania, called "The Tavern Over Ye Water." It had been first erected because the citizens of Bethlehem, being of the Moravian faith, were not too keen on taking into their homes strangers who might not respect their religion or their Moravian ways of life, or, on the other hand, who should not be compelled to join in. So the inn flourished for many years on this basis.

Here's Ray Russell's nice putdown of the way that some drinkers flaunt mindless circumlocution and pretentious euphemism. Such misplaced verbal elegance isn't, of course, confined to the bar. It turns our old people into senior citizens and our garbage men into sanitation engineers.

name your poison

by ray russell

PLAIN TALK does not a highball make, nor honest words a lush. Which, translated, means that we (yes, you and I) are probably inhibited about calling liquor and drinking and drunkenness by their real names.

You think not? Perhaps the point can be best illustrated by an imaginative, though not wholly imaginary, scene featuring—you guessed it: a certain girthful, sable-jawed author, now engaged in casting pearls before Hollywood swine, and sometimes vice versa.

We fade in as I enter my office in the writers' building of (Blank) Studios in my customary manner: palsied, yawning, skin chalky, eyes bright as two raw oysters. Noting all this, my alert and pretty secretary asks, "Want some coffee?"

"Please."

"Large?"

"*S'il vous plait.*"

"Black?"

"*Por favor.*"

"And would you prefer Anacin, Bufferin or Excedrin?"

"One of each flavor, please."

"Chaser?"

"Alka-Seltzer on the rocks."

"Pretty rough night, eh?" she observes patronizingly.

"I really Tied One On," I admit.

"What? Aren't you the fellow who upbraided me the other day about the cowardly use of euphemism, circumlocution, synecdoche, metonymy, and so on?"

"Sure, there's still discrimination, but it is *getting better."*

"I'm the fellow. What about it?"

"Well, why do you say you Tied One On? Why don't you simply admit you were drunk?"

"Because I *wasn't* drunk, smarty-pants, that's why. Not what *I'd* call drunk. I enjoyed a friendly Snort, yes, a Quick One just to Wet the Whistle; you know, One for the Road. . . ."

"You mean a glass of liquor?"

"I'll ignore that. There's nothing wrong with Bending the Elbow a bit with one's cronies to Repair the Tissues, getting together to Refresh the Inner Man by the time-honored custom of Hoisting a Few. . . ."

NAME YOUR POISON   43

"Oh, now it's a few. A few what? A few Nips, Swigs, Shots, Slugs, Jolts?"

"If you will."

"Of Booze, Hooch, Sauce, Snake Oil, Redeye? Or maybe you only drank wine—oops, I mean the Grape."

"Are you *quite* finished?" I ask icily.

She isn't. "Was it an Eye Opener you had or a Pick-Me-Up? I suppose it was too early for a Nightcap. Or maybe you like to say the Cup That Cheers?"

"I wouldn't be caught dead saying the Cup That Cheers. And speaking of cups, brighteyes, what about that coffee?"

"You wouldn't prefer the Hair of the Dog?"

"Woman! You try my patience! Begone!"

She vanishes, the fear of God plainly in her. I sink into my swivel chair, fall asleep and promptly dream an unusual dream. I dream a girl walks into my office carrying the complete works of Benjamin

---

A well-dressed gentleman seated at the bar was quietly guzzling martinis. After finishing each one, he carefully ate the glass and arranged the stems in a neat row. The ninth time this occurred, the bartender could stand it no longer and commented to another customer, "There's a guy who's absolutely nuts."

"He sure is," agreed the other man. "The stems are the best part."

Franklin, in six volumes. Now, my secretary returns, and the sound of her voice awakens me abruptly:

"Here's your coffee. Also your pills. Also the complete works of Benjamin Franklin, in six volumes."

"I didn't ask for—"

"I suggest you read what he has to say in number twelve of the *Dogood Papers.*"

"You. Are. Out. Of. Your. *Mind!* Benjamin Franklin on a Monday morning?"

"It's Tuesday afternoon."

She opens the *Dogood Papers*, and, with rapidly glazing eyes, I skim the words to which she points: "It argues some shame in the drunkards themselves, in that they have invented numberless words and phrases to cover their folly, whose proper significations are harmless, or have no signification at all. They are seldom known to be drunk, though they are very often Boozey, Cogey, Tipsey, Foxed, Merry, Mellow, Fuddled, Groatable, Confoundedly Cut, See Two Moons, or The Sun Has Shown Upon Them; they Clip The King's

English, are Almost Froze, Feverish, In Their Altitudes, Pretty Well Entered—" At this point my eyeballs roll up into my skull of their own accord, and she says, alarmed:

"You worry me. I was going to lunch now, but I'm not sure I should leave you. Will you be all right?"

"Of course I'll be all right! Don't be so damned solicitous!"

"Well, you look sick."

"I am not *sick.* I have a Hangover, which is a very different thing. I'm a little Under the Weather, that's all."

"Just a touch of the Morning After?"

"That's the ticket. The usual Katzenjammers. The Horrors. A Big Head, nothing more. You go to lunch. Go right ahead and gorge yourself, that's quite all right; but in the spirit of reciprocal solicitude, I feel compelled to point out that you've been getting a trifle chunky around the middle; so it might be a good idea to go easy on the calories. Not that *I* mind, but sudden pudginess in girls is often misinterpreted, and people do talk. No, no, don't bother to thank me; it's part of my job to look after the welfare of my little charges. And, speaking of little charges, I assume your relief secretary—your petite, slender relief secretary—stands ready to defend the fort in your absence? Good, fine, excellent. Please inform her that I am not to be disturbed during the next hour for any reason. Got that straight? Swell. Ta-ta, sweetie, and as you walk into the commissary, avert your eyes from the sour-cream cheesecake with strawberry topping—it's murder on the shape."

Her exit is uncharacteristically silent. So is the hour that follows. No phone calls, no visitors, nothing to disturb my rest. I awake much refreshed and very hungry. I lift the phone to order a bit of lunch. It is dead. I jiggle the button. Nothing. Undaunted, I rise and walk to the door. It is locked. Giving vent to strong language, which I will not reproduce here, I fish my office key from my pocket and unlock the door. I am prepared to admonish the relief secretary, but she is not at her desk. In the carriage of the secretarial typewriter is a memo from secretary number one to secretary number two. I take the liberty of reading it:

"White Fang is in a filthy mood today," it reads, "and doesn't want to be disturbed 'for any reason.' I suggest you have the operator put a plug in the switchboard so he can't receive calls and so he won't be tempted to make any, either. We must save him from himself. By the same token, be so good as to lock his door so people won't be wandering in while he's snoring and drooling and making a spectacle of himself. And then, if I were you, I'd take the afternoon off, since there'll be nothing left to do. In the unlikely event that he

"So you thought we were coming up here to drink some spirits, eh, MacGruter?!"

outwits us and gets through to you, do not, under any circumstances, make reference to his delicate condition. If you find you absolutely *must* allude to it, for your own good, use only the following terms, which I have arranged in alphabetical order for your convenience: A Drop Too Much, Bagged, Barreled, Bit of a Glow On, Blasted, Blind, Blotto, Boiled, Buzzed, Cockeyed, Conked, Corked, Corned, Crocked, Feeling No Pain, Floating, Flying High, Fried, Gassed, Greased, Groggy, Half Shot, Has a Snootful, High, Inebriated, In His Cups, Intoxicated, Jagged, Juiced, Listing to the Leeward, Lit, Loaded, Looped, On a Bender, On a Spree, On a Tear, On a Toot, Paralyzed, Petrified, Pickled, Pie-Eyed, Piffed, Pifflicated, Plastered, Plotched, Plotzed, Polluted, Puddled, Saturated, Seeing Double, Shellacked, Skunked, Smashed, Snoggered, Sozzled, Spiffed, Squiffed, Stewed, Stiff, Stinko, Stoned, Swacked, Tanked, Three Sheets to the Wind, Tiddly, Tight and Under the Influence. Those are off the top of my head, but if you need more, consult Ben Franklin's 12th *Dogood Paper* and Roget's *Thesaurus.* I don't want to give you the impression that our boy is a drunkard—he may be a Bibber, a Lush, a Rummy, a Toper, a Tippler, a Tosspot, a Souse, a Soak and a Sot; he may be Off the Wagon, but nothing worse than that. However. . . .''

My reading is interrupted by her return from lunch. Immediately I pantomime looking through her desk for rubber bands.

"They're in the top left drawer," she says flatly.

"Hm? Ah, there you are. Have you eaten your fill?"

"No," she pouts. "I decided you were serious about my getting chunky. I had a watercress salad."

"That's terrible! I apologize! You're not getting chunky at all!"

"You're just saying that."

"I'll prove it. Come out to dinner with me tonight."

"Why should I?"

" 'Dost thou love life? Then do not squander time. Who pleasure gives shall joy receive.' That's why. You know who uttered that utterance?"

"Benjamin Franklin?"

"Absolutely correct, Pick you up about seven at your place. Better yet, six-thirty. That'll give me time to sample your liquor before we—"

"Sample what?"

"*What I mean is,*" I say loudly, to placate the gods of euphemism, "it's been a hell of a day, and I feel the need of a Wee Dram before dinner."

come, thou monarch of the vine

by william shakespeare

(1564–1616)

COME, thou monarch of the vine,
 Plumpy Bacchus with pink eyne!
 In thy vats our cares be drown'd,
With thy grapes our hairs be crown'd:
 Cup us, till the world go round,
 Cup us, till the world go round!

What is the influence of the stars on gentlemen in bars? Are you a Scorpio with vodka rising? Read what the heavens have to say about your thirst.

the signs
you drink under

by philip allingham

December 23–January 20

CAPRICORN

Being thorough, you drink with care and concentration, and the wine list to you is a fascinating inventory, not an embarrassment. Bouquet you appreciate with love and complete understanding. Unlikely to mix your drinks unwisely, you take infinite pains to obtain the right mixture of friends and liquor. Toping has little effect on your sense of humor, which is adequate but never boisterous. The women are discriminate tipplers, taking their sherry pale and dry and their drinking seriously.

January 21–February 19

AQUARIUS

Though your sign is the Water Carrier, your appreciation of good, strong liquor becomes intelligently acute with the years. Innately inquisitive, your thirst for knowledge is unquenchable. The out-of-the-way tavern and little-known drink have a strong appeal. But a streak of cussedness may reveal itself toward the evening's end, and your reaction toward the landlord's final call is always uncertain. Irrational by nature, your behavior is unpredictable. Under mental stress have been known to become total abstainers, but a return to right living immediately restores a healthy mind. Women drink fitfully but survive most sessions.

February 20–March 20

PISCES

Poor fish. Your eyes immediately betray the extent of your drinking but your legs seldom let you down. Might tell the story of a broken heart after the "eighth" but normally an intelligent listener. Have a fishlike thirst which is never sated. Shorts are your forte. Advised to explore the possibilities of vodka as a base. Adaptable, you find solace in odd company and places but prefer drinking in plush surroundings. With a glass in your hand you have few inhibitions. The women possess that rare tranquillity so ideal for long, becalmed hours of serious wine drinking.

March 21–April 20

ARIES

Can drink almost anything—and usually do. Judgment sound enough but your constitution even better. A youthful accomplishment to sample every bottle behind the bar in turn brings you to middle-age with a solid background based on liquid foundations. Likes beer best, but brandy proves a solace in the winter of your years. A trifle blunt at your soberest, diplomacy is not increased when in your cups. Never intimidated, your way of dealing with a wine waiter most effective. The women take the initiative when ordering wine, especially when not paying for it.

April 21–May 21

TAURUS

Neither Bacchus nor pep-talks needed to boost your ego. Happily your opinion of yourself is shared by others. Can introduce originality and good humor into any gathering, appearing bibacious in good company though drinking in moderation. Though positive in many ideas and prejudices, you have an open mind and mouth regarding drink. Have been known to order whatever the others are having rather than exert the effort of making a decision. Might pay out of turn—knowingly—rather than break up a session. Taurus women often appear to choose their drinks by colors.

May 22–June 22

GEMINI

The dual streak in your nature gives you a capacity for doing two things at once—and drinking is one of them. You never lose your powers of reasoning, champagne being your best stimulant with some of your brightest ideas having, perhaps, originated from the cellars of Rheims. There is a youthfulness of spirit about you which outlives the night's supply of alcohol. Gemini women are less possessive than most. In many cases, as with port, they improve with keeping.

June 23–July 23

CANCER

The moon gives you a wandering instinct, possibly responsible for your never remaining faithful to one particular hostelry, though your nature is to become deeply attached to people and places. At some time you may be connected with the sea. When you splice the mainbrace you do so wholeheartedly and, even if your longest journey was across the English Channel, you are apt to walk with a distinct nautical gait when three sheets in the wind. Rum is your best beverage. Women drink little themselves but have a gift for choosing good wines and naughty escorts.

July 24–August 23

LEO

Leo is the sign of leadership. You're as liable to start a new fashion in drinks as in everything else. Never lost in moments of emergency, it's you who can produce the corkscrew or the extra guest. Your creative streak produces the best cocktails and the story to top all others. Avoid lonely drinking when you become maudlin rather than mellow. Women born under Leo find it difficult to refuse a loan or a favor. To accept a casual drink might prove expensive.

August 24–September 23

VIRGO

Many total abstainers are born under this sign, but statistics happily reveal that their number is diminishing. You are methodical, perhaps a little too cautious, with a certain faddiness about food and drink. You know your own mind but underestimate your capabilities. Propitious for change—garage the car, order another round, become a good mixer. Postpone your journey.

INNKEEPER'S LIABILITY ACT 1863: The landlord cannot be held responsible for any personal injury to a married man following this advice.

September 24–October 23

LIBRA

Your first drink of the day is probably an Alka-Seltzer; the morning is not your best period. Normally a malleable soul, friendly toward everyone except those connected with the Internal Revenue Service. Quick to see another's point of view or an empty glass, yours is the gift to create harmony. You can hold your liquor, have terrific staying power and resourcefulness, and display great ingenuity in getting a drink at any hour. Women have excellent palates and exciting personalities. Would recognize the subtle qualities of a good Rhine Wine.

October 24–November 22

SCORPIO

You were born to be loved or loathed according to the other person's temperament. A prolific talker and a rather absent-minded drinker, you are sometimes too hurried in emptying your glass and reaching the point of your story. A natural exuberance might endanger your reputation for holding your liquor. A pleasant time is had by almost all, except perhaps when two Scorpios meet. Women cocktail drinkers tick over smoothly on a weak mixture.

SAGITTARIUS

The Archer is the sportsman in the company. No matter how precious the nectar, thimblefuls are hardly adequate. You drink when you're thirsty, and your thirst is a constant companion. Can throw a useful dart, and a convincing line in reminiscences. For everyday drinking your judgment of a vintage port would doubtless be well founded. The women are rarely enthusiastic imbibers but are not without virtues. They display infinite patience with dogs, horses, husbands and all dumb creatures.

Here's a poignantly dated piece, a loving tribute to the place that for many years had been the most proudly traditional saloon in America, McSorley's Old Ale House, the only saloon "where it was possible to relax."

When this splendid bastion of male camaraderie fell to the Women's Liberation Movement in 1970, something very precious died and some of us were led to wonder if the movement was completely devoid of shame. The unique bygone atmosphere of McSorley's is captured for you here by Joseph Mitchell's words and by John Sloan's brush on the cover. You will never find two better pictures of a happy place to drink.

the old house
at home

by joseph mitchell

MCSORLEY'S occupies the ground floor of a red brick tenement at 15 Seventh Street, just off Cooper Square, where the Bowery ends. It was opened in 1854 and is the oldest saloon in New York City. In eighty-eight years it has had four owners—an Irish immigrant, his son, a retired policeman, and his daughter—and all of them have been opposed to change. It is equipped with electricity, but the bar is stubbornly illuminated with a pair of gas lamps, which flicker fitfully and throw shadows on the low, cobwebby ceiling each time someone opens the street door. There is no cash register. Coins are dropped in soup bowls—one for nickels, one for dimes, one for quarters, and one for halves—and bills are kept in a rosewood cashbox. It is a drowsy place; the bartenders never make a needless move, the customers nurse their mugs of ale, and the three clocks on the walls have not been in agreement for many years. The clientele is motley. It includes mechanics from the many garages in the neighborhood, salesmen from the restaurant-supply houses on Cooper Square, truck-drivers from Wanamaker's, internes from Bellevue, students from Cooper Union, and clerks from the row of secondhand bookshops just north of Astor Place. The backbone of the clientele, however, is a rapidly thinning group of crusty old men, predominantly Irish, who have been drinking there since they were youths and now have a proprietary feeling toward the place. Some of them have tiny pensions, and are alone in the world; they sleep in Bowery hotels and spend practically all their waking hours in McSorley's. A few of these veterans clearly remember John McSorley, the founder, who died in 1910 at the age of eighty-seven. They refer to him as Old John, and they like to sit in rickety armchairs around the big belly stove which heats the place, gnaw on the stems of their pipes, and talk about him.

Old John was quirky. He was normally affable but was subject to spells of unaccountable surliness during which he would refuse to answer when spoken to. He went bald in early manhood and began wearing scraggly, patriarchal sideburns before he was forty. Many photographs of him are in existence, and it is obvious that he had a lot of unassumed dignity. He patterned his saloon after a public house he had known in Ireland and originally called it the Old House at Home; around 1908 the signboard blew down, and when he ordered a new one he changed the name to McSorley's Old Ale House. That is still the official name; customers never have called it anything but McSorley's. Old John believed it impossible for men to drink with tranquillity in the presence of women; there is a fine back room in the saloon, but for many years a sign was nailed on the street door, saying, "Notice. No Back Room in Here for Ladies." In McSorley's entire history, in fact, the only woman customer ever willingly admitted was an addled old peddler called Mother Fresh-Roasted, who claimed her husband died from the bite of a lizard in Cuba during the Spanish-American War and who went from saloon to saloon on the lower East Side for a couple of generations hawking

---

Storming into the frontier saloon, the fervid temperance evangelist boomed, "Repent, you vile sinners! Drinking that noxious fluid will send you all to hell. Join with me—all of you who want to go to heaven stand on this side."

All but one drunk staggered to his side. To the holdout, the evangelist shouted, "Don't you want to go to heaven?"

"No, I don't," replied the drunk.

"You mean to tell me that you don't want to go to heaven when you die?" asked the astonished evangelist.

"Oh," the drunk replied, "when I *die*. I thought you were making up a load right now."

---

peanuts, which she carried in her apron. On warm days, Old John would sell her an ale, and her esteem for him was such that she embroidered him a little American flag and gave it to him one Fourth of July; he had it framed and placed it on the wall above his brass-bound ale pump, and it is still there. When other women came in, Old John would hurry forward, make a bow, and say, "Madam, I'm sorry, but we don't serve ladies." If a woman insisted, Old John would take her by the elbow, head her toward the door, and say,

*"Tom, I gotta take a leak. Are there any women's libbers
in the men's john?"*

"Madam, please don't provoke me. Make haste and get yourself off the premises, or I'll be obliged to forget you're a lady." This technique, word for word, is still in use.

In his time, Old John catered to the Irish and German workingmen—carpenters, tanners, bricklayers, slaughter-house butchers, teamsters, and brewers—who populated the Seventh Street neighborhood, selling ale in pewter mugs at five cents a mug and putting out a free lunch inflexibly consisting of soda crackers, raw onions, and cheese; present-day customers are wont to complain that some of the cheese Old John laid out on opening night in 1854 is still there. Adjacent to the free lunch he kept a quart crock of tobacco and a rack of clay and corncob pipes—the purchase of an ale entitled a man to a smoke on the house; the rack still holds a few of the communal pipes. Old John was thrifty and was able to buy the tenement—it is five stories high and holds eight families—about ten years after he opened the saloon in it. He distrusted banks and always kept his money in a cast-iron safe; it still stands in the back room, but its doors are loose on their hinges and there is nothing in it but an accumulation of expired saloon licences and several McSorley heirlooms, including Old John's straight razor. He lived with his family in a flat directly over the saloon and got up every morning at five; he walked to the Battery and back before breakfast, no matter what the weather. He unlocked the saloon at seven, swept it out himself, and spread sawdust on the floor. Until he became too feeble to manage a racing sulky, he always kept a horse and a nanny goat in a stable around the corner on St. Mark's Place. He kept both animals in the same stall, believing, like many horse-lovers, that horses should have company at night. During the lull in the afternoon a stablehand would lead the horse around to a hitching block in front of the saloon, and Old John, wearing his bar apron, would stand on the curb and groom the animal. A customer who wanted service would tap on the window and Old John would drop his currycomb, step inside, draw an ale, and return at once to the horse. On Sundays he entered sulky races on uptown highways.

From the time he was twenty until he was fifty-five, Old John drank steadily, but throughout the last thirty-two years of his life he did not take a drop, saying, "I've had my share." Except for a few experimental months in 1905 or 1906, no spirits ever have been sold in McSorley's; Old John maintained that the man never lived who needed a stronger drink than a mug of stock ale warmed on the hob of a stove. He was a big eater. Customarily, just before locking up for the night, he would grill himself a three-pound T-bone, placing it on a coal shovel and holding it over a bed of oak coals in the back-room fireplace. He liked to fit a whole onion into the hollowed-out heel of a loaf of French bread and eat it as if it were an apple. He had an extraordinary appetite for onions, the stronger the better, and said that "Good ale, raw onions, and no ladies" was the motto of his saloon. About once a month during the winter he presided over an on-the-house beefsteak party in the back room, and late in life he was president of an organization of gluttons called the Honorable John McSorley Pickle, Beefsteak, Baseball Nine, and Chowder Club, which held hot-rock clambakes in a picnic grove on North Brother Island in the East River. On the walls are a number of photographs taken at outings of the club, and in most of them the members are squatting around barrels of ale; except for the president, they all have drunken, slack-mouthed grins and their eyes look dazed. Old John had a bull-frog bass and enjoyed harmonizing with a choir of drunks. His favorite songs were "Muldoon, the Solid Man," "Swim Out, You're Over Your Head," "Maggie Murphy's Home," and

---

It was almost midnight, and the attractive, well-stacked woman had been standing at the bus stop for over half an hour, obviously several martinis past her limit, when up drove a personable-appearing chap with an offer of transportation home. Sliding into the seat beside him, the inebriated miss managed to mumble her address, then slumped drowsily against the fellow's shoulder. Responding to the opportunity, the driver wrapped his free arm around his pretty passenger and pressed her closer to him, proceeding with as personal an appraisal of the terrain as possible without taking his eyes off the road or his other hand off the wheel.

At first she seemed oblivious to what was going on, but then she came to life, exclaiming, "Man, you're passionate!"

Quite naturally flattered by this apparent reference to his romantic technique, he attempted to take further liberties and was promptly greeted with a stinging slap across the face. Stopping the car abruptly, he turned to her angrily and said, "Look, lady, on the one hand you tell me how passionate I am, and with the other you smack me. Why don't you make up your mind?"

"I don't know what you're talkin' about, mishter," came the slurred reply, "but all I was referring to was my house—I said you're pashin' it!"

"Since the Soup House Moved Away." These songs were by Harrigan and Hart, who were then called "the Gilbert and Sullivan of the U.S.A." He had great respect for them and was pleased exceedingly when, in 1882, they made his saloon the scene of one of their slum comedies; it was called "McSorley's Inflation."

Although by no means a handshaker, Old John knew many prominent men. One of his closest friends was Peter Cooper, president of the North American Telegraph Company and founder of Cooper Union, which is a half-block west of the saloon. Mr. Cooper, in his declining years, spent so many afternoons in the back room philosophizing with the workingmen that he was given a chair of his own; it was equipped with an inflated rubber cushion. (The chair is still there; each April 4th for a number of years after Mr. Cooper's death, on April 4, 1883, it was draped with black cloth.) Also, like other steadfast customers, Mr. Cooper had a pewter mug on which his name had been engraved with an icepick. He gave the saloon a life-sized portrait of himself, which hangs over the mantel in the back room. It is a rather appropriate decoration, because, since the beginning of prohibition, McSorley's has been the official saloon of Cooper Union students. Sometimes a sentimental student will stand beneath the portrait and drink a toast to Mr. Cooper.

Old John had a remarkable passion for memorabilia. For years he saved the wishbones of Thanksgiving and Christmas turkeys and strung them on a rod connecting the pair of gas lamps over the bar; the dusty bones are invariably the first thing a new customer gets inquisitive about. Not long ago, a Johnny-come-lately infuriated one of the bartenders by remarking, "Maybe the old boy believed in voodoo." Old John decorated the partition between barroom and back room with banquet menus, autographs, starfish shells, theatre programs, political posters, and worn-down shoes taken off the hoofs of various race and brewery horses. Above the entrance to the back room he hung a shillelagh and a sign: "BE GOOD OR BEGONE." On one wall of the barroom he placed portraits of horses, steamboats, Tammany bosses, jockeys, actors, singers, and statesmen. Around 1902 he put up a heavy oak frame containing excellent portraits of Lincoln, Garfield, and McKinley, and to the frame he attached a brass title tag reading, "THEY ASSASSINATED THESE GOOD MEN THE SKULKING DOGS." On the same wall he hung framed front pages of old newspapers; one, from the London *Times* for June 22, 1815, has in the lower right-hand corner a single paragraph on the beginning of the battle of Waterloo, and another, from the New York *Herald* of April 15, 1865, has a one-column story on the shooting of Lincoln. He blanketed another wall with lithographs and steel engravings. One depicts Garfield's deathbed. Another is entitled "The Great Fight." It was between Tom Hyer and Yankee Sullivan, both bare-knuckled, at Still Pond Heights, Maryland, in 1849. It was won by Hyer in sixteen rounds, and the prize was $10,000. The judges wore top hats. The title tag on another engraving reads, "Rescue of Colonel Thomas J. Kelly and Captain Timothy Deacy by Members of the Irish Revolutionary Brotherhood from the

English Government at Manchester, England, September 18, 1867."
A copy of the Emancipation Proclamation is on this wall; so,
inevitably, is a facsimile of Lincoln's saloon license. An engraving of
Washington and his generals hangs next to an engraving of a
session of the Great Parliament of Ireland. Eventually Old John
covered practically every square inch of wall space between wainscot
and ceiling with pictures and souvenirs. They are still in good
condition, although spiders have strung webs across many of them.
New customers get up on chairs and spend hours studying them.

Although Old John did not consider himself retired until just a few
years before he died, he gave up day-in-and-day-out duty back of the
bar around 1890 and made his son, William, head bartender. Bill
McSorley was the kind of person who minds his own business
vigorously. He inherited every bit of his father's surliness and not
much of his affability. The father was by no means a lush, but the
son carried temperance to an extreme; he drank nothing but tap
water and tea, and bragged about it. He did dip a little snuff. He was
so solemn that before he was thirty several customers had settled
into the habit of calling him Old Bill. He worshipped his father, but
no one was aware of the profundity of his worship until Old John
died. After the funeral, Bill locked the saloon, went upstairs to the
family flat, pulled the shutters to, and did not come out for almost a
week. Finally, on a Sunday morning, gaunt and silent, he came
downstairs with a hammer and a screwdriver and spent the day
painstakingly securing his father's pictures and souvenirs to the
walls; they had been hung hit or miss on wires, and customers had a
habit of taking them down. Subsequently he commissioned a
Cooper Union art teacher to make a small painting of Old John from
a photograph. Bill placed it on the wall back of the bar and thereafter
kept a hooded electric light burning above it, a pious custom that is
still observed.

Throughout his life Bill's principal concern was to keep McSorley's
exactly as it had been in his father's time. When anything had to be
changed or repaired, it appeared to pain him physically. For twenty
years the bar had a deepening sag. A carpenter warned him
repeatedly that it was about to collapse; finally, in 1933, he told the
carpenter to go ahead and prop it up. While the work was in progress
he sat at a table in the back room with his head in his hands and got
so upset he could not eat for several days. In the same year the
smoke- and cobweb-encrusted paint on the ceiling began to flake off
and float to the floor. After customers complained that they were
afraid the flakes they found in their ale might strangle them to death,
he grudgingly had the ceiling repainted. In 1925 he had to switch to

"Get right up there again before you lose your nerve."

earthenware mugs; most of the pewter ones had been stolen by souvenir hunters. In the same year a coin-box telephone, which he would never answer himself, was installed in the back room. These were about the only major changes he ever allowed. Occasionally one of the pictures his father had hung would fall off the wall and the glass would break, and he would fill in the gap. His contributions include a set of portraits of the wives of Presidents through the first Mrs. Woodrow Wilson, a poster of Barney Oldfield in a red racing car, and a poem called "The Man Behind the Bar." He knew this poem by heart and particularly liked the last verse:

When St. Peter sees him coming he will leave the gates ajar,
For he knows he's had his hell on earth, has the man behind the bar.

As a businessman, Bill was anachronous; he hated banks, cash registers, bookkeeping, and salesmen. If the saloon became crowded, he would close up early, saying, "I'm getting too confounded much trade in here." Agents for the brewery from which he bought his ale often tried to get him to open a checking account; he stubbornly continued to pay his ale bills with currency, largely silver. He would count out the money four or five times and hand it to the driver in a paper bag. Bill was an able bartender. He understood ale; he knew how to draw it and how to keep it, and his bar pipes were always clean. In warm weather he made a practice of chilling the mugs in a tub of ice; even though a customer nursed an ale a long time, the chilled earthenware mug kept it cool. Except during prohibition, the rich, wax-colored ale sold in McSorley's always has come from the Fidelio Brewery on First Avenue; the brewery was founded two years before the saloon. In 1934, Bill sold this brewery the right to call its ale McSorley's Cream Stock and gave it permission to use Old John's picture on the label; around the picture is the legend "As brewed for McSorley's Old Ale House." During prohibition McSorley's ale was produced mysteriously in a row of washtubs in the cellar by a retired brewer named Barney Kelly, who would come down three times a week from his home in the Bronx. On these days the smell of malt and wet hops would be strong in the place. Kelly's product was raw and extraordinarily emphatic, and Bill made a practice of weakening it with near beer. In fact, throughout prohibition Bill referred to his ale as near beer, a euphemism which greatly amused the customers. One night a policeman who knew Bill stuck his head in the door and said, "I seen a old man up at the corner wrestling with a truck horse. I asked him what he'd been drinking and he said, 'Near beer in McSorley's.'" The prohibition ale cost fifteen cents, or two mugs for a quarter. Ale now costs a dime a mug.

Bill was big and thick-shouldered, but he did not look strong; he had a shambling walk and a haggard face and always appeared to be convalescing from something. He wore rusty-black suits and black bow ties; his shirts, however, were surprisingly fancy—they were silk, with candy stripes. He was nearsighted, the saloon was always dimly lit, and his most rigid conviction was that drink should not be sold to minors; consequently he would sometimes peer across the bar at a small-sized adult and say, "Won't sell you nothing, bud. Get along home, where you belong." Once he stared for a long time at a corner of the saloon and suddenly shouted, "Take your foot off that table!" Evidently he had been staring at a shadow; no one was sitting in the corner. Bill was tyrannical. Reading a newspaper, he would completely disregard a line of customers waiting to be served. If a man became impatient and demanded a drink, Bill would look up angrily and shout obscene remarks at him in a high, nasal voice. Such treatment did not annoy customers but made them snicker; they thought he was funny. In fact, despite Bill's bad disposition, many customers were fond of him. They had known him since they were young men together and had grown accustomed to his quirks.

Having wandered helplessly into a blinding snowstorm, Sam, a notorious drinker, was greatly relieved to see a sturdy St. Bernard dog bounding toward him with a keg of brandy strapped to his collar. "At last," cried Sam, "man's best friend—and a great big dog, too!"

They even took a wry sort of pride in him, and when they said he was the gloomiest, or the stingiest, man in the Western Hemisphere there was boastfulness in their voices; the more eccentric he became, the more they respected him. Sometimes, for the benefit of a newcomer, one of these customers would show Bill off, shouting, "Hey, Bill, lend me fifty dollars!" or "Hey, Bill, there ain't no pockets in a shroud!" Such remarks usually provoked an outburst of gamy epithets. Then the customer would turn proudly to the newcomer and say, "See?" When prohibition came, Bill simply disregarded it. He ran wide open. He did not have a peephole door, nor did he pay protection, but McSorley's was never raided; the fact that it was patronized by a number of Tammany politicians and minor police officials probably gave it immunity.

Bill never had a fixed closing hour but locked up as soon as he began to feel sleepy, which was usually around ten o'clock. Just before closing he would summon everybody to the bar and buy a round. This had been his father's custom and he faithfully carried it on, even though it seemed to hurt him to do so. If the customers were slow about finishing the final drink, he would cough fretfully once or twice, then drum on the bar with both fists and say, "Now, see here, gents! I'm under no obligoddamnation to stand here all night while you baby them drinks." Whenever Bill completely lost his temper he would jump up and down and moan piteously. One night in the winter of 1924 a feminist from Greenwich Village put on trousers, a man's topcoat, and a cap, stuck a cigar in her mouth, and entered McSorley's. She bought an ale, drank it, removed her cap, and shook her long hair down on her shoulders. Then she called Bill a male chauvinist, yelled something about the equality of the sexes, and ran out. When Bill realized he had sold a drink to a woman, he let out a cross between a moan and a bellow and began to jump up and down as if his heels were on fire. "She was a woman!" he yelled. "She was a goddamn woman!"

Bill was deaf, or pretended to be; even so, ordinary noises seemed to bother him unduly. The method he devised to keep the saloon tranquil was characteristic of him. He bought a fire-alarm gong similar to those used in schools and factories and screwed it to the seven-foot-tall icebox behind the bar. If someone started a song, or if the old men sitting around the stove began to yell at each other, he would shuffle over to the gong and give the rope a series of savage jerks. The gong is there yet and is customarily sounded at a quarter to midnight as a warning that closing time is imminent; the customers grab their ears when it goes off. Bill was consistent in his aversion to noise; he didn't even like the sound of his own voice. He was able to go for days without speaking, answering all questions with a snort or a grunt. A man who drank in McSorley's steadily for sixteen years once said that in that time Bill spoke exactly four intelligible words to him. They were "Curiosity killed the cat." The man had politely asked Bill to tell him the history of a pair of rusty convict shackles on the wall. He learned later that a customer who had fought in the Civil War had brought them back from a Confederate prison in Andersonville, Georgia, and had given them to Old John as a souvenir.

Bill would sometimes take an inexplicable liking to a customer. Around 1911 a number of painters began hanging out in McSorley's. Among them were John Sloan, George Luks, Glenn O. Coleman, and Stuart Davis. They were all good painters, they didn't put on

"One Scotch and soda, and one Gatorade."

airs, and the workingmen in the saloon accepted them as equals. One night, Hippolyte Havel, the anarchist, came in with the painters. Havel was a long-haired, myopic, gentle-mannered Czech whose speeches often got him in trouble with the police. Even Bill was curious about him. "What's that crazy-looking feller do for a living?" he asked one of the painters. Playing safe, the painter said Havel was a politician, more or less. Havel liked the place and became a steady customer. Most nights, after making a fiery speech in Union Square, he would hurry down to McSorley's. To the amazement of the old-timers, a strong friendship grew up between him and Bill, who was a Tammany Democrat and an utter reactionary; no one was ever able to figure out the basis of the friendship. Bill called the anarchist Hippo and would let him have credit up to two dollars; other customers were not allowed to charge so much as a nickel cigar. Bill had an extremely vague idea about Havel's politics. Charles Francis Murphy, the Tammany boss, occasionally dropped in, and once Bill told Havel he was going to speak a good word to the boss for him. "Maybe he'll put you in line for something," Bill said. The anarchist, who thought no man was as foul as a Tammany boss, smiled and thanked him. A police captain once took it upon himself to warn Bill against Havel. "You better keep your eyes on that long-haired nut," he said. "Why?" asked Bill. The question annoyed the police captain. "Hell fire, man," he said, "Havel's an anarchist! He's in favor of blowing up every bank in the country." "So am I," said Bill. Bill's friendship for Havel was extraordinary in every way. As a rule, he reserved his kindness for cats. He owned as many as eighteen at once and they had the run of the saloon. He fed them on bull livers put through a sausage grinder and they became enormous. When it came time to feed them, he would leave the bar, no matter how brisk business was, and bang on the bottom of a tin pan; the fat cats would come loping up, like leopards, from all corners of the saloon.

Bill had been married but was childless, and he used to say, "When I go, this place goes with me." In March, 1936, however, he changed his mind—why, no one knows—and, to the surprise of the veteran customers, sold both saloon and tenement to Daniel O'Con-

---

A rather inebriated fellow on a bus was tearing up a newspaper into tiny pieces and throwing them out the window.

"Excuse me," said the woman sitting next to him, "but would you mind explaining why you're tearing up that paper and throwing the pieces out the window?"

"It scares away the elephants," said the drunk.

"I don't see any elephants," said the woman, smiling.

"Effective, isn't it?" said the drunk.

---

nell, an old policeman, who, since 1900, had spent most of his leisure at a table in the back room. O'Connell retired from the Department two days before he purchased the saloon. He was the kind of man of whom people say, "If he can't speak a good word about you, he won't speak a bad one." He was almost as proud of the saloon's traditions as Bill and willingly promised he would make no changes; that was one of the conditions of the sale. Almost from the day Bill sold out, his health began to fail. He took a room in the house of a relative in Queens. Sometimes, in the afternoon, if the weather was good, he would shuffle into the bar, a sallow, disenchanted old man, and sit in the Peter Cooper chair with his knotty hands limp in his lap. For hours he would sit and stare at the painting of Old John. The customers were sure he was getting ready to die, but when he came in they would say, "You looking chipper today, Billy boy," or something like that. He seemed grateful for such remarks. He rarely spoke, but once he turned to a man he had known for forty years and said, "Times have changed, McNally." "You said it, Bill," McNally replied. Then, as if afraid he had been sentimental, Bill coughed, spat, and said, irrelevantly, "The bread you get these days, it ain't fit to feed a dog." On the night of September 21, 1938, barely thirty-one months after he quit drawing ale, he died in his sleep. As close as his friends could figure it, his age was seventy-six.

The retired policeman made a gentle saloonkeeper. Unlike Bill, he would never throw a quarrelsome drunk into the street but would try to sober him up with soup. "If a man gets crazy on stuff I sold him, I can't kick him out," he said one day. "That would be evading my responsibility." He was proprietor for less than four years. He died in December, 1939, and left the property to a daughter, Mrs. Dorothy O'Connell Kirwan. A young woman with respect for tradition, Mrs. Kirwan has chosen to remain completely in the background. At first customers feared that she would renovate the place, but they now realize that this fear was groundless. "I know exactly how my father felt about McSorley's," Mrs. Kirwan once said, "and so long as I am owner, no changes will be made. I won't even change the rule against women customers." She herself visits the saloon only on Sunday nights after hours. She appointed a brother-in-law, Joe Nida, manager and retained the old bartenders, Eddie Mullins and Joe Martoccio. Mike, the cook, a Ukrainian, was also retained. The most important member of the staff of McSorley's, however, is not actually an employee. His name is Tommy Kelly, and he is called Kelly the Floorwalker. He is not related to Barney Kelly, the prohibition brewer. Since around 1904, Kelly has acted as a sort of volunteer potboy and master of ceremonies. During prohibition, Bill had him on the payroll, but most of the time he has worked for the pleasure of it. When business is brisk, he totes mugs from the bar to the tables; also, he makes an occasional trip to the butcher for Mike. In the winter he keeps a fire going. When he shows up, around 8:30 A.M., he is just a sad-eyed little man with a hangover, but by noon lukewarm ale has given him a certain stateliness; by six he is in such a good humor that he stands near the door and shakes hands with incoming customers just as if he were the proprietor. Strangers think he is the proprietor and call him Mr. McSorley. Technically, Kelly is a truck-driver, but he always says business is slow in his line. Once, for a brief period, he took a job as night clerk in a funeral parlor in Brooklyn, quitting because a corpse spoke to him. "This dead feller looked up at me and told me to take my hat off indoors," Kelly says. In one way or another, death pops up repeatedly in Kelly's talk. Each morning, Mullins, the bartender, asks him how he feels. If he doesn't feel so good, he says, "I'm dead, but I just won't lie still." Otherwise he says, "For a old drunk with one leg in the grave and not a penny to his name, I can't complain."

To a steady McSorley customer, most other New York saloons seem feminine and fit only for college boys and women; the atmosphere in them is so tense and disquieting that he has to drink himself into a coma in order to stand it. In McSorley's the customers are self-sufficient; they never try to impress each other. Also, they are not competitive. In other saloons if a man tells a story, good or bad, the man next to him laughs perfunctorily and immediately tries to tell a better one. It is possible to relax in McSorley's. For one thing, it is dark and gloomy, and repose comes easy in a gloomy place. Also, there is a thick, musty smell that acts as a balm to jerky nerves; it is really a rich compound of the smells of pine sawdust, tap drippings, pipe tobacco, coal smoke, and onions. A Bellevue interne once said that for many mental disturbances the smell in McSorley's is more beneficial than psychoanalysis.

At midday McSorley's is crowded. The afternoon is quiet. At six it fills up with men who work in the neighborhood. Most nights there are a few curiosity-seekers in the place. If they behave themselves and don't ask too many questions, they are tolerated. The majority of them have learned about the saloon through John Sloan's paintings. Between 1912 and 1930, Sloan did five paintings, filled with detail, of the saloon—"McSorley's Bar," which shows Bill presiding majestically over the tap and which hangs in the Detroit Institute of Arts; "McSorley's Back Room," a painting of an old workingman sitting at the window at dusk with his hands in his lap, his pewter mug on the table; "McSorley's at Home," which shows a group of argumentative old-timers around the stove; "McSorley's Cats," in which Bill is preparing to feed his drove of cats; and "McSorley's, Saturday Night," which was painted during prohibition and shows Bill passing out mugs to a crowd of rollicking customers. Every time one of these appears in an exhibition or in a newspaper or magazine, there is a rush of strangers to the saloon. "McSorley's Bar" was reproduced in Thomas Craven's "A Treasury of Art Masterpieces," which came out in 1939, and it caused hundreds to go and look the place over. There is no doubt that McSorley's has been painted more often than any other saloon in the country. Louis Bouché did a painting, "McSorley's," which is owned by the University of Nebraska. A painting, "Morning in McSorley's Bar," by a ship's purser named Ben Rosen won first prize in an exhibition of art by merchant seamen in February, 1943. Reginald Marsh has done several sketches of it. In 1939 there was a retrospective exhibition of Sloan's work in Wanamaker's art department, and a number of McSorley patrons attended it in a body. One asked a clerk for the price of "McSorley's Cats." "Three thousand

"I'd be careful if I were you buddy—that's the bartender's wife. . . ."

dollars," he was told. He believed the clerk was kidding him and is still indignant. Kelly likes the Sloan paintings but prefers a golden, corpulent nude which Old John hung in the back room many years ago, right beside Peter Cooper's portrait. To a stranger, attracted to the saloon by a Sloan painting, Kelly will say, "Hey, Mac, if you want to see some real art, go look at the naked lady in the back room." The nude is stretched out on a couch and is playing with a parrot; the painting is a copy, probably done by a Cooper Union Student, of Gustave Courbet's "La Femme au Perroquet." Kelly always translates this for strangers. "It's French," he says learnedly. "It means 'Duh Goil and duh Polly.'"

McSorley's bar is short, accommodating approximately ten elbows, and is shored up with iron pipes. It is to the right as you enter. To the left is a row of armchairs with their stiff backs against the wainscoting. The chairs are rickety; when a fat man is sitting in one, it squeaks like new shoes every time he takes a breath. The customers believe in sitting down; if there are vacant chairs, no one ever stands at the bar. Down the middle of the room is a row of battered tables. Their tops are always sticky with spilled ale. In the center of the room stands the belly stove, which has an isinglass door and is exactly like the stoves in Elevated stations. All winter Kelly keeps it red hot. "Warmer you get, drunker you get," he says. Some customers prefer mulled ale. They keep their mugs on the hob until the ale gets as hot as coffee. A sluggish cat named Minnie sleeps in a scuttle beside the stove. The floor boards are warped, and here and there a hole has been patched with a flattened-out soup can. The back room looks out on a blind tenement court. In this room are three big, round dining-room tables. The kitchen is in one corner of the room; Mike keeps a folding boudoir screen around the gas range, and pots, pans, and paper bags of groceries are stored on the mantelpiece. While he peels potatoes, he sits with early customers at a table out front, holding a dishpan in his lap and talking as he peels. The fare in McSorley's is plain, cheap and well cooked. Mike's specialties are goulash, frankfurters, and sauerkraut, and hamburgers blanketed with fried onions. He scribbles his menu in chalk on a slate which hangs in the barroom and consistently misspells four dishes out of five. There is no waiter. During the lunch hour, if Mike is too busy to wait on the customers, they grab plates and help themselves out of the pots on the range. They eat with their hats on and they use toothpicks. Mike refers to food as "she." For example, if a customer complains that the goulash is not as good as it was last Wednesday, he says, "No matter how not as good she is, she's good enough for you."

The saloon opens at eight. Mike gives the floor a lick and a promise and throws on clean sawdust. He replenishes the free-lunch platters with cheese and onions and fills a bowl with cold, hard-boiled eggs, five cents each. Kelly shows up. The ale truck makes its delivery. Then, in the middle of the morning, the old men begin shuffling in. Kelly calls them "the steadies." The majority are retired laborers and small businessmen. They prefer McSorley's to their homes. A few live in the neighborhood, but many come from a distance. One, a retired operator of a chain of Bowery flophouses, comes in from Sheepshead Bay practically every day. On the day of his retirement, this man said, "If my savings hold out, I'll never draw another sober breath." He says he drinks in order to forget the misery he saw in his flophouses; he undoubtedly saw a lot of it, because he often drinks twenty-five mugs a day, and McSorley's ale is by no means weak. Kelly brings the old men their drinks. To save him a trip, they usually order two mugs at a time. Most of them are quiet and dignified; a few are eccentrics. Some years ago one had to leap out of the path of a speeding automobile on Third Avenue; he is still furious. He mutters to himself constantly. Once, asked what he was muttering about, he said, "Going to buy a shotgun and stand on

 As the cop helped the bruised and battered bibber up from the pavement in front of the bar, he asked, "Can you describe the man who hit you?"
"Oh, yes," said the drunk. "That's just what I was doing when he hit me."

Third Avenue and shoot at automobiles." "Are you going to aim at the tires?" he was asked. "Why, hell no!" he said. "At the drivers. Figure I could kill four or five before they arrested me. Might kill more if I could reload fast enough."

Only a few of the old men have enough interest in the present to read newspapers. These patrons sit up front, to get the light that comes through the grimy street windows. When they grow tired of reading, they stare for hours into the street. There is always something worth looking at on Seventh Street. It is one of those East Side streets completely under the domination of kids. While playing stickball, they keep great packing-box fires going in the gutter; sometimes they roast mickies in the gutter fires. Drunks reel over from the Bowery and go to sleep in doorways, and the kids give them hotfoots with kitchen matches. In McSorley's the free-lunch platters are kept at the end of the bar nearer the street door, and several times every afternoon kids sidle in, snatch handfuls of cheese and slices of onion, and dash out, slamming the door. This never fails to amuse the old men.

The stove overheats the place and some of the old men are able to sleep in their chairs for long periods. Occasionally one will snore, and Kelly will rouse him, saying, "You making enough racket to wake the dead." Once Kelly got interested in a sleeper and clocked him. Two hours and forty minutes after the man dozed off, Kelly became uneasy—"Maybe he died," he said—and shook him awake. "How long did I sleep?" the man asked. "Since the parade," Kelly said. The man rubbed his eyes and asked, "Which parade?" "The Paddy's Day parade, two years ago," Kelly said scornfully. "Jeez!" the man said. Then he yawned and went back to sleep. Kelly makes jokes about the constancy of the old men. "Hey, Eddie," he said one morning, "old man Ryan must be dead!" "Why?" Mullins asked. "Well," Kelly said, "he ain't been in all week." In summer they sit in the back room, which is as cool as a cellar. In winter they grab the chairs nearest the stove and sit in them, as motionless as barnacles, until around six, when they yawn, stretch, and start for home, insulated with ale against the dreadful loneliness of the old. "God be wit' yez," Kelly says as they go out the door.

ballade of liquid refreshment

by e.c. bentley

LAST night we started with some dry vermouth;
Some ancient sherry, with a golden glow;
Then many flagons of the soul of fruit
Such as Burgundian vineyards only grow;
A bottle each of port was not *de trop*;
And then old brandy till the east was pink
—But talking makes me hoarse as any crow,
Excuse me while I go and have a drink.

Some talk of Alexander: some impute
Absorbency to Mirabeau-Tonneau;
Some say that General Grant and King Canute,
Falstaff and Pitt and Edgar Allan Poe,
Prince Charlie, Carteret, Hans Breitmann—so
The list goes on—they say that these could clink
The can, and take their liquor—*A propos*!
Excuse me while I go and have a drink.

Spirit of all that lives, from God to brute,
Spirit of love and life, of sun and snow,
Spirit of leaf and limb, of race and root,
How wonderfully art thou prison'd! Lo!
I quaff the cup, I feel the magic flow,
And Superman succeeds to Missing Link,
(I say, "I quaff"; but am I quaffing? No!
Excuse me while I go and have a drink.)

Hullo there, Prince! Is that you down below,
Kicking and frying by the brimstone brink?
Well, well! It had to come some time, you know.
Excuse me while I go and have a drink.

Robert Benchley was a funny man with a profound scholarly interest in drinking. The title of this Benchley piece reminds me of my favorite cocktail-hour story. When he visited a certain club in New York one afternoon, Harry Truman asked for a bourbon and water.

"I'm sorry," said the head of the club. "The bar doesn't open till five o'clock."

"Fine," said Truman, "bring me the drink. It's five o'clock somewhere."

For those of you who happen to be under 65, the word repeal in Benchley's piece refers to the repeal of the 18th Amendment, which prohibited the manufacture and sale of intoxicating liquor in America. Hard as it is to believe, drinking was once unconstitutional.

cocktail hour

by robert benchley

IT IS all very well for New York and other large cities to go cosmopolitan in their new-found freedom, and to sit at sidewalk cafes in the Springtime, sipping their *aperitifs* and *demiblondes.* That was to be expected with Repeal.

But I must, merely as a passer-by, ask ladies who run tea-rooms not to put signs reading: "Cocktail Hour" in the windows of their tea-shops at two o'clock in the afternoon. Two P.M. is *not* "cocktail hour," no matter how you look at it. The very suggestion is terrifying.

How would you like to be walking along a perfectly normal street, with the hot sun beating down on your new straw hat and a rather heavy corned-beef-hash-with-poached-egg from luncheon keeping step with you, and suddenly to look up and see, pasted on the window of a tea-shop, a sign reading "Cocktail Hour"? I am just putting the question to you as man to man.

If two P.M. is "cocktail hour" in a tea-shop, what do you suppose four-thirty P.M. is? No wonder those shops close early. By nine they would be a shambles.

Do you suppose that the habitues of these otherwise respectable places begin looking at their watches along about one-thirty, just as they are finishing lunch, and say to each other: "Almost cocktail time at the tea-room!" making a little ceremony of it, the way other people do at five-thirty? It can't be very formal, with so many going right back to work afterward. Just regular business clothes, probably. There'll be only the regular bunch there. You know, the cocktail crowd!

Unless a stop is put to this strange perversion of daytime hours, we shall soon be seeing little signs pasted in the window of our favorite breakfast counter reading: "Have you had your matutinal absinthe and wheatcakes?" or "When you hear the signal, the time will be exactly ten forty-five A.M. Time for our Special Chartreuse and Brandy Whooperoo!"

If the tea-rooms conducted by ladies want to celebrate "cocktail hour" at two P.M. that is their own business, of course, but they ought not to be so doggy about it. They should quite frankly come out with signs saying: "Pick-Me-Up Hour! Whisky Sours and Bismarck Herring for Receding Heads!" or "Don't try to last the afternoon out in your condition. A Silver Fizz will at least keep your hat on." Don't be so delicate in the matter. Come right out for the Hangover Trade.

But please, *please*, don't ask us older boys to look at signs reading "Cocktail Hour" just as we are going back to work from lunch. We have got men's work in the world to do.

now i'm resolved to love no more

by alexander brome

(1620–1666)

NOW I'm resolved to love no more,
    But sleep by night, and drink by day;
Your coyness, Chloris, pray give o'er,
    And turn your tempting eyes away.
From ladies I'll withdraw my heart,
And fix it only on the quart.

I'll place no happiness of mine
    A puling beauty still to court,
And say she's glorious and divine—
    The vintner makes the better sport;
And when I say, my dear, my heart,
I only mean it to the quart.

Love has no more prerogative
    To make me desperate courses take,
Nor me t'an hermitage shall drive,
    I'll all my vows to th' goblet make;
And if I wear a capuchoone,
It shall a tankard be or none.

'Tis wine alone that cheers the soul,
    But love and ladies make us sad;
I'm merry when I court the bowl,
    While he who courts the madam's mad;
Then ladies wonder not at me,
For you are coy but wine is free.

The literature of hangovers is small. In fact, this is all I was able to find. But happily it is enough. It is also unnecessary if you read the piece that follows it, for Dr. Amis is as profound about prevention as he is about cure.

the hangover

by kingsley amis

THERE are poems and songs about drinking, of course, but none to speak of about getting drunk, let alone having been drunk. Novelists go into the subject more deeply and extensively, but tend to straddle the target, either polishing off the hero's hangover in a few sentences or, so to speak, making it the whole of the novel. In the latter case, the hero will almost certainly be a dipsomaniac, who is not as most men are and never less so than on the morning after. This vital difference, together with much else, is firmly brought out in Charles Jackson's marvelous and horrifying *The Lost Weekend*, still the best fictional account of alcoholism I have read.

A few writers can be taken as metaphorically illuminating the world of the hangover while ostensibly dealing with something else. Parts of Dostoevsky can be read in this way. Some of Poe's tales convey perfectly the prevailing gloomy uneasiness and sudden fits of outlandish dread so many of us could recognize, and Poe himself had a drinking problem; contrary to popular belief, he was not a dipsomaniac, but his system was abnormally intolerant of alcohol, so that just a couple of slugs would lay him on his back, no doubt with a real premature-burial of a hangover to follow. Perhaps Kafka's story *The Metamorphosis*, which starts with the hero waking up one morning and finding he has turned into a man-sized cockroach, is the best literary treatment of all. The central image could hardly be better chosen, and there is a telling touch in the nasty way everybody goes on at the chap. (I can find no information about Kafka's drinking history.)

It is not my job, or anyway I absolutely decline, to attempt a full, direct description of the metaphysical hangover: no fun to write or read. But I hope something of this will emerge by implication from my list of countermeasures. Before I get on to that, however, I must deal with the physical hangover, which is in any case the logical one to tackle first, and the dispersal of which will notably alleviate the other—mind and body, as we have already seen, being nowhere more intimately connected than in the sphere of drink. Here, then, is how to cope with

THE PHYSICAL HANGOVER

1. Immediately on waking, start telling yourself how lucky you are to be feeling so bloody awful. This, known as George Gale's Paradox, recognizes the truth that if you do *not* feel bloody awful after a hefty night then you are still drunk, and must sober up in a waking state before hangover dawns.

2. If your wife or other partner is beside you, and (of course) is willing, perform the sexual act as vigorously as you can. The exercise will do you good, and—on the assumption that you enjoy sex—you will feel toned up emotionally, thus delivering a hit-and-run raid on your metaphysical hangover (M.H.) before you formally declare war on it.

Warnings: (i) If you are in bed with somebody you should not be in bed with, and have *in the least degree* a bad conscience about this, abstain. Guilt and shame are prominent constituents of the M.H.,

 A friend of ours has come up with the David and Goliath cocktail—a small one and you're stoned.

and will certainly be sharpened by indulgence on such an occasion.

(ii) For the same generic reason, do not take the matter into your own hands if you awake by yourself.

3. Having of course omitted to drink all that water before retiring, drink a lot of it now, more than you need to satisfy your immediate thirst. Alcohol is a notorious dehydrant, and a considerable part of your physical hangover (P.H.) comes from the lack of water in your cells.

At this point I must assume that you can devote at least a good part of the day to yourself and your condition. Those who inescapably have to get up and do something can only stay in bed as long as they

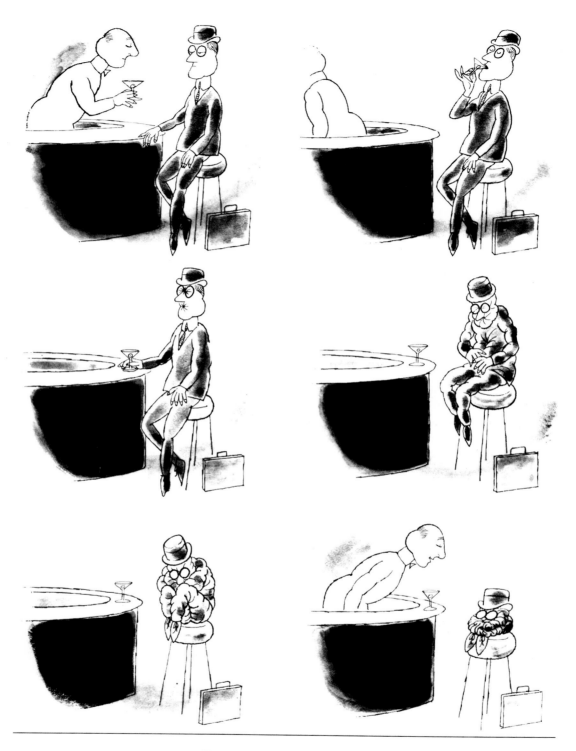

"Dry enough for you, sir?"

dare, get up, shave, take a hot bath or shower (more of this later), breakfast off an unsweetened grapefruit (m.o.t.l.) and coffee, and clear off, with the intention of getting as drunk at lunchtime as they dare. Others can read on—but let me just observe in passing that the reason why so many professional artists drink a lot does not necessarily have very much to do with the artistic temperament, etc. It is simply that they can afford to, because they can normally take a large part of a day off to deal with the ravages. So, then,

4. Stay in bed until you can stand it no longer. Simple fatigue is another great constituent of the P.H.

5. Refrain at all costs from taking a cold shower. It may bring temporary relief, but in my own and others' experience it will give your M.H. a tremendous boost after about half an hour, in extreme cases making you feel like a creature from another planet. Perhaps this is the result of having dealt another shock to your already shocked system. The ideal arrangement, very much worth the trouble and expense if you are anything of a serious drinker, is a shower fixed over the bath. Run a bath as hot as you can bear and lie in it as long as you can bear. When it becomes too much, stand up and have a hot shower, then lie down again and repeat the sequence. This is time well spent.

Warning: Do not do this unless you are quite sure your heart and the rest of you will stand it. I would find it most disagreeable to be accused of precipitating your death, especially in court.

6. Shave. A drag, true, and you may well cut yourself, but it is a calming exercise and will lift your morale (another sideswipe at your M.H.).

7. Whatever the state of your stomach, do not take an alkalizing agent such as bicarbonate of soda. There is some of this in most hangover remedies but not enough to do you any harm, and the bubbling is cheerful. Better to take unsweetened fruit juice or a grapefruit without sugar. The reasoning behind this, known as Philip Hope–Wallace's Syndrome, is that your stomach, on receiving a further dose of acid, will say to itself, "Oh, I see: we need more alkaline," and proceed to neutralize itself. Bicarbonate will make it say, "Oh, I see: we need more acid," and do you further damage.

If you find this unconvincing, take heed of what happened one morning when, with a kingly hangover, I took bicarbonate with a vodka chaser. My companion said "Let's see what's happening in your stomach," and poured the remnant of the vodka into the remnant of the bicarbonate solution. The mixture turned black and gave off smoke.

8. Eat nothing, or nothing else. Give your digestion the morning

off. You may drink coffee, though do not expect this to do anything for you beyond making you feel more wide-awake.

9. Try not to smoke. That nicotine has contributed to your P.H. is a view held by many people, including myself.

10. By now you will have shot a good deal of the morning. Get through the rest of it somehow, avoiding the society of your fellows. Talk is tiring. Go for a walk, or sit or lie about in the fresh air. At eleven or so, see if you fancy the idea of a Polish Bison (hot Bovril and vodka). It is still worth while without the vodka. You can start working on your M.H. any time you like.

11. About 12:30, firmly take a hair (or better, in Cyril Connolly's phrase, a tuft) of the dog that bit you. The dog, by the way, is of no particular breed: there is no obligation to go for the same drink as the one you were mainly punishing the night before. Many will favor the Bloody Mary; others swear by the Underburg. For the ignorant, this is a highly alcoholic bitters rather resembling Fernet Branca, but in my experience more usually effective. It comes in miniature bottles holding about a pub double, and should be put down in one. The effect on one's insides, after a few seconds, is rather like that of throwing a cricket-ball into an empty bath, and the

---

The wife of a friend of ours purchased a rather large grandfather clock at an auction and then sent her unhappy husband to pay for it and carry the damn thing home. To make matters worse, the husband had been to a formal dinner earlier in the evening and was still wearing his full-dress suit. He was having some difficulty with the unwieldy mechanism even before he met the drunk staggering in the opposite direction. They collided, and the husband fell backward to the sidewalk, the clock on top of him.

"Why in blazes don't you watch where you're going!" the angry husband demanded.

The drunk shook his head dazedly, looked at the man in the full-dress suit and at the grandfather clock that lay across him.

"Why don't you wear a wrishwatch like everybody elsh?" he inquired.

---

resulting mild convulsions and cries of shock are well worth witnessing. But thereafter a comforting glow supervenes, and very often a marked turn for the better. By now, one way or another, you will be readier to face the rest of mankind and a convivial lunchtime can well result. Eat what you like within reason, avoiding anything greasy or rich. If your P.H. is still with you afterwards, go to bed.

Before going on to the M.H., I will, for completeness' sake, mention three supposed hangover cures, all described as infallible by those who told me about them, though I have not tried any of the three. The first two are hard to come by.

12. Go down the mine on the early-morning shift at the coal-face.

13. Go up for half an hour in an open airplane, needless to say with a non-hungover person at the controls.

14. Known as Donald Watt's Jolt, this consists of a tumbler of some sweet liqueur, Bénédictine or Grand Marnier, taken in lieu of breakfast. Its inventor told me that with one of them inside him he once spent three-quarters of an hour at a freezing bus-stop "without turning a hair." It is true that the sugar in the drink will give you energy and the alcohol alcohol.

At this point, younger readers may relax the unremitting attention with which they have followed the above. They are mostly strangers to the M.H. But they will grin or jeer at their peril. Let them rest assured that, as they grow older, the M.H. will more and more come to fill the gap left by their progressively less severe P.H. And, of the two, incomparably the more dreadful is

THE METAPHYSICAL HANGOVER

1. Deal thoroughly with your P.H.

2. When that ineffable compound of depression, sadness (these two are not the same), anxiety, self-hatred, sense of failure and fear for the future begins to steal over you, start telling yourself that what you have is a hangover. You are not sickening for anything, you have not suffered a minor brain lesion, you are not all that bad at your job, your family and friends are not leagued in a conspiracy of barely maintained silence about what a shit you are, you have not come at last to see life as it really is, and there is no use crying over spilt milk. If this works, if you can convince yourself, you need do no more, as provided in the markedly philosophical

He who truly believes he has a hangover has no hangover.

3. If necessary, then, embark on *either* the M.H. Literature Course *or* the M.H. Music Course *or* both in succession (not simultaneously). Going off and gazing at some painting, building or bit of statuary might do you good too, but most people, I think, will find such things unimmediate for this—perhaps any—purpose. The structure of both Courses, HANGOVER READING and HANGOVER LISTENING, rests on the principle that you must feel worse emotionally before you start to feel better. A good cry is the initial aim.

Begin with verse, if you have any taste for it. Any really gloomy stuff that you admire will do. My own choice would tend to include the final scene of *Paradise Lost*, Book XII, lines 606 to the end, with what is probably the most poignant moment in all our literature coming at lines 624–6. The trouble here, though, is that today of all days you do not want to be reminded of how inferior you are to the man next door, let alone to a chap like Milton. Safer to pick somebody less horribly great. I would plump for the poems of A. E. Housman and/or R. S. Thomas, not that they are in the least interchangeable. Matthew Arnold's *Sohrab and Rustum* is good, too, if a little long for the purpose.

Switch to prose with the same principles of selection. I suggest Alexander Solzhenitsyn's *One Day in the Life of Ivan Denisovitch.* It is not gloomy exactly, but its picture of life in a Russian labor camp will do you the important service of suggesting that there are plenty of people about who have a bloody sight more to put up with than you (or I) have or ever will have, and who put up with it, if not cheerfully, at any rate in no mood of self-pity.

Turn now to stuff that suggests there may be some point to living after all. Battle poems come in rather well here: Macaulay's *Horatius*, for instance. Or, should you feel that this selection is getting a bit British (for the Roman virtues Macaulay celebrates have very much that sort of flavor), try Chesterton's *Lepanto*. The naval victory in 1571 of the forces of the Papal League over the Turks and their allies was accomplished without the assistance of a single Anglo-Saxon (or Protestant). Try not to mind the way Chesterton makes some play with the fact that this was a victory of Christians over Moslems.

By this time you could well be finding it conceivable that you might smile again some day. However, defer funny stuff for the moment. Try a good thriller or action story, which will start to wean you from self-observation and the darker emotions: Ian Fleming, Eric Ambler, Gavin Lyall, Dick Francis, Geoffrey Household, C. S. Forester (perhaps the most useful of the lot). Turn to comedy only after that; but it must be white—i.e. not black—comedy: P. G. Wodehouse, Stephen Leacock, Captain Marryat, Anthony Powell (not Evelyn Waugh), Peter De Vries (not *Blood of the Lamb*, which, though very funny, has its real place in the tearful category, and a distinguished one). I am not suggesting that these writers are comparable in other ways than that they make unwillingness to laugh seem a little pompous and absurd.

HANGOVER LISTENING

Here, the trap is to set your sights too high. On the argument tentatively advanced against unduly great literature, give a wide berth to anyone like Mozart. Go for someone who is merely a towering genius. Tchaikovsky would be my best buy in this department, and his Sixth Symphony (the *Pathétique*) my individual selection. After various false consolations have been set aside, its last movement really does what the composer intended and, in an amazingly non-dreary way, evokes total despair: sonic M.H. if ever I heard it.

Alternatively, or next, try Tchaikovsky's successor, Sibelius. *The Swan of Tuonela* comes to mind, often recommended though it curiously is (or was in my youth) as a seduction background-piece. (Scope for a little article there.) Better still for our purpose, I think, is the same composer's incidental music to Maeterlinck's play, *Pelléas and Mélisande*: not to be confused with Debussy's opera of that name. The last section of the Sibelius, in particular, carries the ever-so-slightly phoney and overdone pathos that is exactly what you want in your present state.

If you can stand vocal music, I strongly recommend Brahms's *Alto Rhapsody*—not an alto sax, you peasant, but a contralto voice, with

 A drunk and his inebriated friend were sitting at a bar. "Do you know what time it is?" asked the drunk. "Sure," said the friend. "Thanks," said the drunk.

men's choir and full orchestra. By what must be pure chance, the words sung, from a—between you and me, rather crappy—poem of Goethe's, *Harzreise im Winter*, sound like an only slightly metaphorical account of a hangover. They begin, *"Aber abseits wer ist's?"*—all right, I am only copying it off the record sleeve; they begin, "But who is that (standing) apart? His path is lost in the undergrowth," and end with an appeal to God to "open the clouded vista over the thousand springs beside the thirsty one in the desert." The last phrase gets a lot in. You can restore some of your fallen dignity by telling yourself that you too are a *Duerstender in der*

Wueste. This is a piece that would fetch tears from a stone, especially a half-stoned stone, and nobody without a record of it in his possession should dare to say that he likes music. The Kathleen Ferrier version is still unequaled after twenty years.

Turn now to something lively and extrovert, but be careful. Quite a lot of stuff that appears to be so at first inspection has a nasty habit of sneaking in odd blows to the emotional solar plexus; ballet music (except Tchaikovsky) and overtures to light operas and such are safer—Suppé, if you have no objection to being reminded of school sports days here and there, is fine. Or better, Haydn's *Trumpet Concerto*, which would make a zombie dance.

Jazz is not much good for your M.H., and pop will probably worsen your P.H. But if you really feel that life could not possibly be gloomier, try any slow Miles Davis track. It will suggest to you that, however gloomy life may be, it cannot possibly be as gloomy as Davis makes it out to be. There is also the likely bonus to be gained from hearing some bystander refer to Davis as Miles instead of Davis. The surge of adrenalin at this piece of trendy pseudo-familiarity will buck up your system, and striking the offender to the ground will restore your belief in your own masculinity, rugged force, etc.

Warning: Make quite sure that Davis's sometime partner, John Coltrane, is not "playing" his saxophone on any track you choose. *He* will suggest to you, in the strongest terms, that life is exactly what you are at present taking it to be: cheap, futile and meaningless.

how not
to get drunk

by kingsley amis

THIS is strictly two topics—how to keep sober (or at least relatively in control) at a drinking party, and what to avoid with the morning after in mind—but they overlap so much in practice that I will treat them under the same heading.

Staying away altogether is a stratagem sometimes facetiously put forward at the outset of such discussions as these. To move at once to the realm of the practical, *eating* has much to be said for it. As well as retarding (though not preventing) the absorption of alcohol, food will slow up your drinking rate, not just because most people put their glasses down while actually chewing, but because you are now satisfying your appetite by eating rather than drinking: hunger makes you drink more than you otherwise would. According to some, oily foods are the most effective soakers-up of the drink already in your stomach, but others point to the risk of upsetting a digestion already under alcoholic attack.

There is a great deal of folklore about *taking some olive oil or milk* before joining the party. This will indeed retard absorption of alcohol, but, as before, it will all get to you in the end. Do not, in any case, overdo the fatty prelude. An acquaintance of mine, led astray by quantitative thinking, once started the evening with a tumbler of olive oil, following this up with a dozen or so whiskies. These, after a couple of hours of nibbling at the film of mucilage supposedly lining his stomach, finally broke through in a body and laid him on the floor of the saloon bar of the Metropole Hotel, Swansea, fortunately after I had left. I would be chary of this tactic. The principle does, however, work well the other way round. In the middle of a greasy

The Vodka Drinker.

meal, a quick neat double brandy certainly seems to hose down your stomach wall and give you heart and strength to continue eating.

Diluting your drinks sounds a good idea to many, and will help to reverse the dehydration that all alcohol brings, so that you will be better off next day. But, again, the alcohol itself will get to you in full. Nor is it true (in my experience, at least) that a double Scotch, say,

---

 Maybe you heard about the drunk who was staggering through the park and saw a young athlete practicing pushups. "Washamatter, Mac?" inquired the lush. "Lose your girl?"

---

diluted with a lot of soda takes longer to put down than the same with a little, so reducing your effective intake. The opposite of all this is truer. Spirits distilled out at 70° British proof, which are what you will usually meet, are too strong in the neat state to be wholly absorbed by the system; a proportion is eventually passed without ever having reached you. Dilution with just less than an equal amount of water is the point at which all the alcohol will enter your bloodstream—a fact known, without benefit of science, to Scotch and Irish drinkers for two centuries. So, in fact, spirit-bibbers should try *drinking neat un-iced spirits*, a practice so grueling that their actual intake is almost bound to drop too.

I pass over such unhelpful prescriptions as *being tall and fat*; it is nevertheless true that your degree of drunkenness depends on a proportion between how much you drink and how large a frame you have to spread it over, with the result that big men, other things being equal, can take more than small men. Other things, of course, never are equal, though there is not much that can be done about them either. *Not being tired, not being depressed, not being specially elated*—these and other negative states will also stiffen your resistance to alcohol, but I know they do not descend at will. It can be said, however, not very cheeringly, that you should watch your drinking rate when you are tired, depressed, etc., (in fact always, because x drinks drunk in y minutes are more potent than x drinks drunk in $2y$ minutes).

Fatigue is an important element in the hangover, too. Alcohol gives you energy, or, what is hard to distinguish from it, the illusion of energy, and under its influence you will stand for hours at a stretch, throw yourself about, do exhausting imitations, perhaps fight a bit, even, God help you, dance. This will burn up a little alcohol, true, but you will pay for it next morning. A researcher is supposed once to have measured out two identical doses of drink, put the first lot down at a full-scale party and the second, some evenings later, at home with a book, smoking the same number of cigarettes on each occasion and going to bed at the same time. Result, big hangover and no hangover respectively. *Sitting down whenever possible*, then, will help you, and so *a fortiori*, will *resisting the temptation to dance*, should you be subject to such impulses.

An equally unsurprising way of avoiding fatigue is *going to bed in reasonable time*, easily said, I know, but more easily done, too, if you allow the soporific effects of drink to run their natural course. This means staying away from stimulants, and that means *avoiding coffee*, both on its own and with liquor poured into it: the latter, by holding you up with one hand while it pastes you at leisure with the other, is the most solidly dependable way I know of ensuring a fearful tomorrow. Hostesses, especially, should take note of this principle, and cut out those steaming midnight mugs which, intended to send the company cheerfully on its way, so often set the tongues wagging and the Scotch circulating again.

Avoiding things can hardly help coming up more than once in the present connection. To proceed, then: *avoiding very strong drinks* is more than the piece of padding it may seem. The alcoholic strength or proof of a wine, spirit, etc., is not a straightforward index of its power to intoxicate. The relationship is non-linear, or, if you must have everything spelled out, the graph plotting proof against kick is not straight. Above the standard strength of spirits it bends sharply upward, so that for instance green Chartreuse, which is distilled out at 96° proof, is not just a bit over a third as strong again as, say, a gin at 70°, but several times stronger in its effect.

I once shared a half-litre bottle of Polish Plain Spirit (140° proof) with two chums. I only spoke twice, first to say, "Cut out that laughing—it can't have got to you yet," and not all that much later to say, "I think I'll go to bed now."

Hand in hand with this warning comes one about *avoiding sweet drinks*. These play hell with you next day; I forget why, but I remember how. So go carefully, at least, with Southern Comfort, a delicious compound of old bourbon whiskey, oranges and peaches that tips the scales at 87.7° proof.

Avoiding unfamiliar drinks is my final interdiction. Here, again, I mean more than just steering clear of Malagasy malaga, St. Peter Port port-type and such, at any rate when you are not in a mood of pure curiosity and cold sober. A friend reports seeing a Highland sergeant, weaned on a bottle of Scotch a day, pass out in his chair after his first-ever half-dozen glasses of table wine. I asked if he was shamming, and was told that his mates were kissing his girl over his recumbent form, which was felt to clinch matters. It is as if—and in the always subjective, idiosyncratic context of drink it need only be as if—body and mind together develop a tolerance to your usual potation, a kind of self-conferred immunity. Do not test this hypothesis too rigorously.

I suppose I cannot leave this topic without reciting the old one about *drinking a lot of water and taking aspirin and/or stomach powders before you finally retire.* It is a pretty useless one as well as an old one because, although the advice is perfectly sound, you will find next morning that you have not followed it. Alternatively, anyone who can summon the will and the energy and the powers of reflection called for has not reached the state in which he really needs the treatment.

After all these bans and discouragements I will throw in one crumb, or tot, of comfort. I am nearly (yes, nearly) sure that mixing your drinks neither makes you drunker nor gives you a worse time the following day than if you had taken the equivalent dosage in some single form of alcohol. After three dry martinis and two sherries and two glasses of hock [Rhine wine] and four of burgundy and one of Sauternes and two of claret and three of port and two brandies and three whiskies-and-soda and a beer, most men will be very drunk and will have a very bad hangover. But might not the quantity be at work here? An evening when you drink a great deal will also be one when you mix them.

Well—if you want to behave better and feel better, the only absolutely certain method is *drinking less.* But to find out how to do *that,* you will have to find a more expert expert than I shall ever be.

well, at least it's not prohibition

IN CALIFORNIA, it's against the law to enter a tavern on horseback.

In Hawaii, you can't whistle in any place that serves drinks.

In St. Louis, it's illegal for anyone but a workingman to sit on a curb and drink beer from a bucket.

In Las Vegas, an ordinance prohibits singing in a public barroom.

And in Cleveland, it's illegal for two men to drink out of the same whiskey bottle and get drunk at the same time.

The Sherry Sipper.

Friar's Song

by William Makepeace Thackeray

(1811–1863)

SOME love the matin-chimes, which tell
    The hour of prayer to sinner;
But better far's the midday bell,
    Which speaks the hour of dinner;
For when I see a smoking fish,
    Or capon drowned in gravy,
Or noble haunch on silver dish,
    Full glad I sing my Ave.

My pulpit is an alehouse bench,
    Whereon I sit so jolly;
A smiling rosy country wench,
    My saint and patron holy.
I kiss her cheek so red and sleek,
    I press her ringlets wavy,
And in her willing ear I speak,
    A most religious Ave.

And if I'm blind, yet Heaven is kind,
    And holy saints forgiving;
For sure he leads a right good life,
    Who thus admires good living.
Above, they say, our flesh is air,
    Our blood celestial ichor:
Oh, grant! 'mid all the changes there,
    They may not change our liquor!

When someone tells you "Skoal!" have you ever wanted to smile and say, "Now what the hell do you mean by that?" Well, here's a delightful history of toasting by humorist William Iversen that will enable you to go one up on the skoalers and even top the L'Chaim boys.

I'm still smiling over Iversen's passage about The Star-Spangled Banner *being an old drinking song. It turns out that even before 1814, people were standing up for this music—or trying to.*

a short history of
toasts and toasting

by william iversen

CHEERS! Prosit! Skoal! ¡Salud! Bottoms up! Here's how! *Na Zdorovje! Okole Maluna!* Down the hatch! *A votre santé!* Lang may your lum reek! *Oogy Wawa!* and Here's to it!

Ranging at random from High German to colloquial Scotch on the rocks, such are some of the innumerable sentiments and exclamations drinking men have used to salute their fellow booze buffs in the ancient and well-nigh universal custom of toasting—a gracious practice which the 18th Century wit Richard Brinsley Sheridan gaily hailed as "an excuse for the glass" and the 17th Century Puritan William Prynne glumly denounced as "a kind of shoehorn to draw on drink in great abundance."

Tugging on our own merry mukluks and dipping into a few well-aged volumes of liquid lore, we soon learn that most of mankind has traditionally drunk "health" and that the idea of drinking a "toast" is peculiar to those who quaff and converse in English.

As a matter of sober fact, even the English drank nothing but health until the latter part of the 17th Century. Prior to that time a toast was only a slice of lightly browned bread that people ate for breakfast, just as they do today—with the singular exception that a bit of toast was often floated in a tankard or bowl of warm, spiced ale to provide a morsel of solid nourishment. In the earliest historical account of how the word *toast* came to be associated with the ritual of drinking to someone's health, Richard (*The Spectator*) Steele reported, in 1709, that the expression first came into vogue among the hard-drinking blue bloods of the Restoration, who were wont to resort to the city of Bath to soak up the fashionable mineral waters in an atmosphere of wine, women and whist. "It happened," as Steele explained in the *Tatler*, "that on a publick Day a celebrated Beauty of those Times was in the Cross Bath, and one of the Crowd of her Admirers took a Glass of the Water in which the Fair one stood, and drank her Health to the Company. There was in the Place a gay

---

 There's nought, no doubt, so much the spirit calms
As rum and true religion.

—LORD BYRON

Fellow, half-fuddled, who offered to jump in, and swore, Tho' he liked not the Liquor, he would have the Toast. He was opposed in his Resolution; yet this whim gave Foundation to the present Honor which is done to the Lady we mention in our Liquors, who has ever since been called a Toast."

According to the 11th edition of the *Encyclopaedia Britannica*, the "custom of drinking 'health' to the living is probably derived from the ancient religious rite of drinking to the gods and the dead. The Greeks and Romans at meals poured out libations to their gods, and at ceremonial banquets drank to them. . . ." In distilling this information down into a couple of quick verbal jiggers, *Britannica* allows several essential facts to evaporate, however. In a libation, for example, a given quantity of liquor is poured out on the ground as a sacrifice to a deity, while in drinking to someone's health the liquor goes gliding down the drinker's own throat. The Greek and Roman custom of passing around a "cup to the good spirit," furthermore, is believed to have originated with the "cup of salvation" that was religiously quaffed by the ancient Hebrews, whose drinking vessels were often smashed on the ground to prevent their being defiled by secular use—a practice that led to the traditional Jewish wedding custom of shattering the glass from which the bride and groom have drunk.

The custom of raising a glass aloft in honor of the person being toasted is also attributed to the early Greeks, who were wine-guzzling health addicts of heroic capacity. To the old Greek ritual of drinking to every god in the Parthenon, Roman revelers added a rousing "three times three" in honor of the Graces and Muses and pledged their loyalty to Caesar by downing a cup for each letter in the emperor's name—a stupefying custom that was also employed in toasting one another's mistresses.

One English historian maintains that it was the Roman conquerors who taught ancient Britons "to drink healths to the Emperor, and to toast the reigning belles with brimming bumpers." Actually, though, the Romans had very little to teach the booze-thirsty barbarians of the North, who had been belting down liquid tributes to gods, chieftains, kinsmen and chums since the prehistoric discovery that the fermentation of honeycombs in water would produce a kind of beer called "mead." The Norse Valhalla, for instance, was hardly more than a heavenly beer hall where the spirits of deserving heroes quaffed health through all eternity, and one of the most ancient of all toasting terms—"skoal," or *skål*—survives from the grisly and forgotten age when Norse warriors drank victorious toasts from the *skalle*, or "skull," of a slain enemy. In like manner, the English word *health* stems from the Old Norse greeting *Heill!* which also gave us "hail," "heal," "hale" and "whole." From the Norsemen's *Ves heill!* or "Be thou well!" came the Anglo-Saxon toast, *Wes hāl!* which the hale-and-hardy English eventually slurred into "wassail."

The festive custom of wassailing antedates Christmas by many centuries, however, and is believed to have evolved from the northerners' midwinter fertility rites, in which bands of boozy celebrants trooped through the forests and made libations of ale, mead or hard cider to restore the dormant fertility of fruit trees.

Whether held on Twelfth Night, New Year's or Christmas Eve, the chief feature of the feast was the bowl of wassail, in which the ancient fruit-and-livestock theme was further evidenced by the addition of roasted crab apples to the brew and the fact that the warm and comforting concoction was affectionately known as "lamb's wool." In a rhymed recipe for this traditional yuletide treat, the poet Herrick directed 17th Century wassailmen to "crown the bowl full with gentle lamb's wooll,"

> *Adde sugar, nutmeg and ginger,*
> *With store of ale too;*
> *And thus ye must doe,*
> *To make the wassaile a swinger.*

Long before Herrick hipped to the ginger-and-apples bit, the pagan toasts of the northern Europeans had been adapted to Christian devotions, and the health that was once drunk to mythical nature gods was now addressed to the Savior and all the saints and angels. Gallic health to the pope was drunk "to the good Father," or *au bon Père*, which the English called drinking "a bumper," and the old wassailing songs set a joyous precedent for the first Christmas carols—the earliest of which often imposed the obligation to drink or be damned.

Since no true Christian could refuse to drink to the saints or the "Christ Mass," which was Christmas, toasting and wassailing soon made drunkenness as obligatory as it had ever been in the heathen days of yore and gore.

Though the celebration of Christmas was sanctimoniously avoided in Puritan New England, the "Saints" of Massachusetts displayed a most decided preference for beer over water and were not above drinking health whenever it suited their purpose. While excessive drinking was discouraged and punished, New England fanaticism was never as well organized as that of the puritanical Scots of Fife, who in 1650 established a special morals squad "to take notice of all disorderly walkers . . . swearers, haunters of alehouses, especially at unreasonable hours and long sitters there and drinkers of healths."

In the early 18th Century the loyal toasts of Englishmen, at home

---

 "If I had a thousand sons, the first human principle I would teach them should be to forswear thin potations."

—WILLIAM SHAKESPEARE
(Falstaff, *Henry IV, Part 2*)

---

and abroad, were offered to the health of middle-aged Queen Anne. It was on the occasion of the queen's birthday in the year 1714 that Samuel Sewall, then justice of the Superior Court of Massachusetts, was roused from his fireside at the ungodly hour of 9:00 P.M. to quell "the Disorders at the Tavern at the Southend." Arriving at the house in question with a constable and party of three, Sewall found "much Company" who "refus'd to go away." They said they were there "to drink the Queen's Health," he confided to his sympathetic diary, "and they had many other Healths to drink. Call'd for more Drink: drank to me, and I took notice of the Affront. . . . Mr. John Netmaker drank the Queen's Health to me. I told him I drank none; upon that he ceas'd. Mr. Brinley put on his Hat to affront me. I made him take it off. I threaten'd to send some of them to prison; that did not move them. . . . Not having Pen and Ink, I went to take their Names with my Pencil, and not knowing how to Spell their Names, they themselves of their own accord writ them. Mr. Netmaker,

"I'll drink to that!"

reproaching the Province, said they had not made one good Law."

Mr. Netmaker and his health-quaffing cronies were sentenced to pay a fine of five shillings each—a mild enough penalty by the older Puritan standards. But Samuel Sewall was still burdened by his self-confessed error in condemning the many innocent victims of the Salem witch trials in 1692. A man of disturbingly human contrasts, he was also the author of the first plea against Negro slavery to be published in the colonies and determined wooer of comely widows. Though he refused to drink the health of Queen Anne, he often drank wine with Mrs. Denison and exchanged amorous courtesies of the glass with Madam Winthrop: "She drank to me, I to her. . . . She had talk'd of Canary, her Kisses were to me better than the best Canary. . . ."

Imported Canary wine was too high-line for the purses of most colonial Americans, who drank their toasts with a variety of home-made brews. There were hard cider and metheglin (made of honey, yeast and water), perry (made from pears) and peachy (made from peaches). Other alcoholic curiosities were made from leaves, bark, berries, beans, roots and cornstalks. In an old sing-along favorite, the courageous colonists proudly claimed:

> Oh, we can make liquor to sweeten our lips
> Of pumpkins, of parsnips, of walnut-tree chips

Gourds and coconut shells supplemented bowls, beakers and tankards as basic equipment for the drinking of colonial health. But "there was no attempt made to give separate drinking cups of any kind to each individual at the table," Alice M. Earle, the author of *Home Life in Colonial Days*, noted at the close of the last century. "Even when tumbler-shaped glasses were seen in many houses . . . they were of communal size—some held a gallon—and all drank from the same glass. The great punch bowl, not a very handy vessel to handle when filled with punch, was passed up and down as freely as though it were a loving cup, and all drank from its brim. . . ."

At Harvard and Yale this was the original college bowl game, later immortalized by a Dartmouth man in the *Hanover Winter Song:* "Ho, a song by the fire! (Pass the pipes, fill the bowl!) Ho, a song by the fire! With a Skoal. . . ." Sarah Kemble Knight, who was said to be Benjamin Franklin's old schoolteacher, watched the communal cup go round a Yankee tavern board and described the drinkers as "being typed by the Lipps to a pewter engine." Her star pupil, the Sage of Philadelphia himself, referred to the glass-passing custom in an original *Drinking Song* dedicated to the proposition "that Virtue and Safety in Wine-bibbing's found,"

> *While all that drink Water deserve to be drown'd.*
> *So for Safety and Honesty put the Glass round.*

A few decades later the American toast was not "Safety and Honesty" drunk in mellow wine but "Liberty and Property" drunk in the fiery New England rum that was the alcoholic embodiment of the Spirit of '76. As Catherine Drinker Bowen has pointed out in her study of *John Adams and the American Revolution*, "Liberty and Property" was the password of the entire American rebellion. "Liberty and property were synonymous. . . . What a man owned was his, as his soul was his. No prince, no king, no parliament could take it from him without his consent. . . ."

In virtually every small village the symbolic "liberty pole" was planted outside a tavern that served as headquarters for the Sons of Liberty, whose early toasts were a peculiar mixture of the loyal and the rebellious. When members of the Boston group met at Chase's Distillery in 1769 to celebrate the anniversary of Boston's protest to the Stamp Act, 45 toasts were drunk, commencing with "the King and Queen" and ending with the threat of "strong halters, firm blocks and sharp axes to all such as deserve either!"

In the opinion of the majority, the man most deserving of sharp axes was none other than Governor Bernard, the king's representative in the Province of Massachusetts, who was credited with having introduced a toasting song that was a favorite with American Tories:

> *Here's a health to all those that we love,*
> *Here's a health to all those that love us,*
> *Here's a health to all those that love them that love those*
> *That love those that love them that love us.*

To the modern American drinker this insidious little tongue twister seems sufficient cause for rebellion in itself. In the light of such repeated provocations, we can only marvel at the restraint of those planter patriots who, upon the dissolution of the Virginia House of Burgesses by the crown, retired to the Raleigh Tavern in Williamsburg to drink loyal toasts to the king, the royal family, "the Farmer" and a "Speedy and Lasting Union between Great Britain and her Colonies." The bar tab, which came to 32 shillings 9 pence, was picked up by a committeeman who was understandably destined to become "first in the hearts of his countrymen"—George Washington. "It was," according to his biographer, Frances Rufus Bellamy, "his first expenditure for liberty."

No event in American history has been celebrated by the drinking of quite so many toasts as the winning of the war for independence.

When Congress demobilized the Continental army, Washington's triumphal journey into retirement was the occasion for a series of banquets at which the formal toasts numbered a symbolic 13. At Annapolis Washington added a 14th: "Sufficient Powers to Congress for general purposes!"

While Washington was being toasted as "the Man who Unites all Hearts" and "Columbia's Favorite Son," the members of a convivial London health club, called "The Anacreonitic Society," were meeting at the Crown and Anchor Tavern, where they opened their meetings with raised galsses and the singing of their club song, *To*

 It is the unbroken testimony of all history that alcoholic liquors have been used by the strongest, wisest, handsomest, and in every way best races of all times.

—GEORGE SAINTSBURY

Anacreon in Heaven. The anthem toasted the memory of the Greek poet who had declared life to be an eternal round of healths. The melody, which every American would immediately recognize as that of *The Star-Spangled Banner*, was adapted to Yankee use as a tribute to *Adams and Liberty* and was later used as the musical setting for the stirring stanzas written by Francis Scott Key.

Another 18th Century toasting song, *Auld Lang Syne*, was fated to become the midnight anthem of all English-speaking New Year's Eve celebrants. The melody was supposed to have been borrowed from the music of the Roman Catholic Church and the words copied down by Robert Burns from the lips of an old Scottish singer. In the land of lively jigs and brimming jiggers, the mood of boozy nostalgia was not confined to one night of the year, however. Clannish quaffers were prepared to share "a cup of kindness" at any season and have traditionally saluted each other with practical wishes for "Mair sense and mair silver!" "Health, wealth, wit and meal!"—and that most canny of all alcoholic benedictions, "Lang may your lum reek [or "Long may your chimney smoke"] wi' ither folks' coal!" But, in justice to the Scots, a similar emphasis upon material well-being is to be found in other folk toasts, such as the Irish Gaelic *Sheed Arth!* ("May you always wear silk!").

In the opinion of the Reverend Richard Valpy French, rector of Llanmartin and Wilcrick, who once gave a temperance lecture that was published in 1880 as the first and only history of toasting in the English language, the drinking of health, "especially in Scotch society, was tyrannically enforced." In the early 1800s persons named in a toast were bound to acknowledge the honor "by placing the right hand on the heart, saying in a very distinct and audible voice, and with a smile of gratification on the countenance, 'Your good health,' then drinking off the glass of wine."

When young Victoria inherited the throne in 1837, her swacked and sprawling subjects enthusiastically toasted "the Queen, God bless her!" By 1845 a fad for adding shouts of "huzza" to every toast had become standard procedure. "Nine times nine cheers" were given for "'Er Royal Majesty" and any deserving 'Arry, 'Erbert or Halbert—a noisy ritual that eventually diminished into a restrained 20th Century murmur of "Cheers."

With or without huzzas, the practice of toasting had to be abolished, temperance forces were still insisting a generation later. "Would that the archbishops and bishops of the Church of England would cease to submit to these appendages at public breakfasts, luncheons and dinners," the Reverend French exclaimed from his temperance platform in 1880 and cited, by way of example, a newspaper account of an "educational dinner" at which "'The Royal Family' was drunk; 'Her Majesty's Ministers' were drunk; 'The Houses of Parliament' were drunk; 'The Universities of Scotland' were drunk; 'Popular Education in its extended sense' was drunk; 'The Clergy of Scotland of all Denominations' were drunk; 'The Parish Schoolmasters' were drunk; other parties not named were drunk; 'The Fine Arts' were drunk; 'The Press' was drunk. . . ."

An equally healthful state of affairs had long obtained in democratic America, where, for more than a century, "the president of the United States" was drunk; "the members of both houses of Congress" were drunk; "the American farmer" and "the American eagle" were drunk; "the wives and mothers of all free men" were drunk—together with the governors, legislators, citizens and judiciary of all the several sovereign states. "Drink rum, drink rum, drink rum, by gum, with me," expressed the will of a free and thirsty people whose manifest destiny can be traced through the innumerable slogans and rallying cries that have served Americans as an excuse for a glass, a mug or a gallon jug: "Tippecanoe and Tyler, too!" "Fifty-four forty or fight!" "Remember the Alamo!" "Pike's Peak or bust!" "The Union forever!" "The stars and the bars!" "Remember the *Maine!*" "To hell with the kaiser!" "Happy days are here again!" "Remember Pearl Harbor!" "Keep 'em flying!" "Get America moving again!"

In the days of "wooden ships and iron men," official toasts were in the patriotic vein of naval hero Stephen Decatur's "Our country: in her intercourse with foreign nations may she always be right; but our country, right or wrong!'' But in grogshops along the waterfront the old bosun's toast was more likely to be:

Here's to the ships of our navy,
And the ladies of our land,
May the first be ever well rigged,
And the latter ever well manned!

While a gentleman of the old South might propose a courtly toast "to the ladies," the Irish immigrant of the North was likely to be knocking back a crock of "blue ruin" with "Here's to the flea that jumped over me and bit the behind of me missus!" While literary and social lights of New York and Boston were toasting the delights of sherry with verses from Omar Khayyám, earthy Pennsylvania Dutchmen set the scene for a shot of schnapps with:

So drink ich, so stick ich,
Drink ich net, so stink ich doch,
So ist besser gedrinka und gestunka,
Os net gedrunka, und doch gestunka!

Which may be translated as "If I drink, I stink. If I don't drink, I stink anyway. So it's better to drink and stink, than to *not* drink and stink anyway!" Though the jargon was mostly German, the reasoning was 100-proof American. In the great age of folk toasting that preceded Prohibition, Americans drank to just about every sentiment conceivable and in a wide range of moods. Some toasts were a strange blend of friendliness and hostility:

Here's a toast for you and me:
And may we never disagree;
But, if we do, then to hell with you.
So here's to me!

Some expressed a touching fondness for a few close friends and cherished possessions:

Hail, good old hat, my companion devoted!
Hail, good old shoes, blest deliverers from pain!
Hail, good old glass, my unfailing inspirer!
Hail, good old friends, ne'er appealed to in vain!

Others were frankly Oedipal:

Here's to the happiest days of my life,
Spent in the arms of another man's wife
—My mother!

Some were dependent rather than devoted and raised the thorny question "Is there booze after death?":

Here's to you and you and you!
If I should die and go to Heaven, and not find you,
I would turn around and go to hell,
Just to be with you and you and you!

Others were defiantly fatalistic:

Here's to hell! May the stay there
Be as much fun as the way there!

There were toasts for tightwads:

Lift 'em high and drain 'em dry
To the guy who says, "My turn to buy!"

There were toasts for truculent underachievers:

Here's to the men who lose!
It is the vanquished's praises that I sing,
And this is the toast I choose:
"A hard-fought failure is a noble thing!"

And there was even a short production number for whimsical nature lovers:

A wee little dog passed a wee little tree.
Said the wee little tree, "Won't you have one on me?"
"No," said the little dog, no bigger than a mouse.
"I just had one on the house."

But the favorite toast was still to a woman. To her face, the smooth-toasting ladies' man of the Eighties and Nineties might raise his glass and murmur, "I have known many, liked a few, loved but one, darling—here's to you!" But in the all-male atmosphere of the corner saloon, the same health-hip Lothario could earn comradely guffaws and envious glances with:

Here's to you, and here's to me,
Here's to the girl with the dimpled knee.
Here's to the boy who fastened her garter;
It wasn't much—but a darned good starter!

Another swain, either less fortunate or more truthful, might be moved to sadly declare:

Here's to dear Alice, so sweet and good.
God made Alice—I wish I could!

The Whiskey Drinker.

Which, in turn, might inspire a recitation of:

> *Here's to the girl who lives on the hill.*
> *She won't, but her sister will.*
> *Here's to her sister!*

In the highly agitated opinion of one temperance poet of the early 20th Century, anybody's sister would if she were properly plied with passionate toasts. "Oh, lovely maids!" he expostulated:

> *Never for all Pactolus' wealth,*
> *In wine let lover drink your health!*
> *Beware the traitor who shall dare*
> *For you the cursed draught prepare. . . .*

As the tempo of American drinking began to swing from a wine-and-beery waltz time to a jazzy cocktail quickstep, male toasters contributed to the growing emancipation of women by concocting drafts that would liberate even the most fettered female libido, and boy-girl toasts became more outspokenly sexual. Removing the rakish overseas cap that was part of his World War One uniform, the citizen soldier toasted his sweetheart of the week with a peppy switch on a sentiment that had once made Lord Cockburn limp with nausea:

> *Here's to the wings of love—*
> *May they never moult a feather,*
> *Till my big boots and your little shoes*
> *Are under the bed together!*

Whether she giggled or silently raised her glass to lips that shaped a smile of promise, the soldier's sweetie might complete her patriotic tour of duty with the cordial cuteness of:

> *Here's to the night I met you.*
> *If I hadn't met you, I wouldn't have let you.*
> *Now that I've let you, I'm glad that I met you.*
> *And I'll let you again, I bet you!*

On leave in Paris, doughboys found that French *mesdemoisells* had a rhymed health hint to convey the same hospitable idea:

> *Je vous baisse, je vous amour.*
> *Si voulez vous, je vous encore.*

Which few members of the Signal Corps needed to have decoded as "I kiss you, I love you. If you wish, I'll do it again." The French toast, Yanks soon learned, was not *A votre santé!* or "To your health!" but *A vos amours!*—"To your loves!"—with a regard for the plural that brought French grammar into complete agreement with the facts of French life. "Here's to the girl who gives and forgives and never sells!" a Gallic grenadier would thunder with the aid of English subtitles. "Here's to the man who gets and forgets and never tells!" *A nos femmes, à nos chevaux et à ceux qui les montent!* the cavalryman could be heard to reply: "To our women, our horses and the men who ride them!"

Italian infantrymen toasted and trudged to the tune of *Viva, viva, viva l'amor. . . . Viva la compagnia!* British tommies of the Mid-

---

Three Fingers of Ajax, Please   How old is wine? It was produced in Palestine at least two thousand years before Christ. Biblical references to wine and vineyards are innumerable. In fact, wine apparently was more plentiful than water and was used in the cleaning of houses.

---

dlesex Regiment drank "Here's to the Middlesex! Here's to the fair sex! Here's to the middle of the fair sex!" Battalions who fought their way through Flanders found the friendly Flemings eager to drink *Dat we het nog lang mogen mogen!*—"That we may still like it for a long time!" And troops who went the whole route into Germany found that *Prosit!* was prosaic compared to the boy-girl *Brüderschaft* toast, in which everlasting "brotherhood" was drunk by linking one's drinking arm through that of a frolicsome *Fräulein* for a face-to-face rendition of:

> *Trink, trink, Brüderlein, trink;*
> *Geh' nicht alleine nach Haus!*
> *Meide den Kummer und meide den Schmerz,*
> *Dann ist das Leben ein Scherz!*

This was followed by a most unbrotherly kiss and repeated until both parties were higher than a *Gemütlichkeit*: "Drink, drink, brother dear, drink; do not go home alone! Avoid sorrow and pain, and all your life will be fun."

Willst du Bier, Komm zu mir!—"If you want beer, you must come here!"—was not the slogan of the American Anti-Saloon League, however. When American veterans returned home, they barely had time to say, "Here's mud in your eye!" before Prohibition was upon them, and American toasting was on its way to becoming a lost art.

"Hurray for enjoyment, hurray for fun! We're going home drunk!" is a year-round Portuguese toast that most Americans would openly endorse only at yuletide—the one season of the year when we abandon our usual mumbled monosyllables for the exuberant eloquence of "Merry Christmas!" and "Happy New Year!" Though unsuitable for use in August and inappropriate for weddings and *bar mitzvahs*, "Merry Christmas" and "Happy New Year" are undoubtedly the two jolliest toasts we have and can hold their own with such exotic seasonal toasts as the French *Joyeux Noel!* the Spanish *¡Feliz Navidad!* and the Italian *Buone Natale!*

Depending on where one spends the holidays, the Christmas toast may be *Gledelig Jul!* (Norwegian), *Vroolijk Kerfeest! (Dutch), Wesoł-ych Świąt!* (Polish) or *Mele Kalikimaka!* (Hawaiian).

A Welshman may say:

> *Oes o lwydd gwir sylweddol—a gaffo*
> *'N deg effaith hanfodol—*
> *A Gwynfa 'n ei ran, ar ol,*
> *Yn gu haddef dragwyddol!*

He's just recited a toast to your early success and is offering the wish that paradise may be your everlasting home.

Those who are not conversant in Welsh may make a reasonably appropriate reply by repeating the Albanian for "May you be happy, too!"—*Gëzuar gofsh!*

Should he counter with "*Brromp!*" don't put him down for "Swine drunke." It only means that he's challenging you to a friendly drink in your adopted tongue.

Clink your glass against his with a smart *twange*, bow three times, kiss your fingers, and reply with a resonant "*Brromp pach!*"—"I accept your challenge!"

Here is a grand reminiscence by Mencken about a place called Sunset Park, the most wicked bar in America at the turn of the century.

A master of English prose and German beer, Mencken was one of the greatest drinkers in the history of Baltimore. He was certainly the most cultured one, for he often stayed up all night drinking beer and playing the cello, a double elbow-bending that fills me with awe.

an evening
on the house

by h.l. mencken

IN THE days of trolley parks, now gone forever, there
was almost as much spread between park and park, culturally
speaking, as you will now find between nightclubs. Some, catering
to what was then called the Moral Element, showed all the hallmarks
of Chautauqua, Asbury Park and Lake Mohonk, with nothing
stronger on tap than ginger ale, soda pop and sarsaparilla, and no
divertisement more provocative to the hormones than quoit-pitching
and the flying horses. But in others there was a frank appeal to the
baser nature of mankind, and at the bottom of the scale were some
that, by the somewhat prissy standards of those days, were veritable
sewers of wickedness. One of the latter sort was operated, in the
Baltimore I adorned as a young newspaper reporter, by a cashiered
police sergeant named Julius Olsen—a man who believed, as he
would often say, in living and letting live. His place lay at the
terminus of a Class D trolley line that meandered down the harbor
side to the shore of one of the affluents of the Patapsco River. Most
of his customers, however, did not patronize this trolley line, which
was outfitted with senile cars that often jumped the track, and shook
the bones out of their passengers when they didn't. Indeed, it was
rare to encounter an actual Baltimorean in the place, which had the
name of Sunset Park. Nearly all the males who frequented it were
sailors from ships berthed along or anchored in the river, and
nine-tenths of the females were adventuresses from either the
Norfolk, Virginia, region, then famous throughout the Eastern
seaboard for its levantine barbarities, or the lower tier of Pennsylvania counties, where the Vice Trust, backed by Wall Street,
maintained agents in every hamlet.

If there was any among the lady visitors to Sunset who had not lost her honest name long before she ever saw it, the fault was not Julius Olsen's for he had a ground rule rigidly excluding all others. Every evening at eight o'clock he would take his place at the garish entrance to his pleasure ground, and give his eye to each female who presented herself, whether alone or with an escort. If there was anything in her aspect that raised a suspicion of chastity he would challenge her at once, and hold her up at the gate until she convinced him that her looks were false to her inner nature. Once, as I stood there with him—for I greatly admired his insight into such things and was eager to learn its secrets—a young couple got off the trolley car and made as if to enter. To my unpracticed eye they looked to be the run-of-the-mine yahoos and nothing more: I could detect no stigmata of chemical purity in the lady. But Julius saw deeper than I did, and as the couple came abreast of his sentry post his heavy paw

The horse and mule live 30 years
And nothing know of wines and beers.
The goat and sheep at 20 die
And never taste of Scotch or Rye.
The cow drinks water by the ton
And at 18 is mostly done.
The dog at 15 cashes in
Without the aid of rum and gin.
The cat in milk and water soaks
And then in 12 short years it croaks.
The modest, sober, bone-dry hen
Lay eggs for nogs, then dies at 10.
All animals are strictly dry;
They sinless live and swiftly die;
But sinful, ginful, rum-soaked men
Survive for three score years and ten.
And some of them, a very few,
Stay pickled till they're 92.

ANON.,
quoted in Arnold Silcock's *Verse and Worse*

fell upon the shoulder of the young man, and his eyebrows drew together in a fearful frown. "What in hell do you mean," he roared, "to bring a nice young girl to such a goddamn dump as this? Ain't you got no goddamn sense at *all*?" The young fellow, amazed and abashed, stood speechless, and Julius bellowed on. "Don't you know," he demanded, "where you are at? Ain't you ever heerd tell of Sunset Park? Goddamn if I ever seen the like of it in all my born

"Make it one for my baby and one more for the road."

days! Do you want a gang of sailors to bash in your head and make off with your girl? What would you have to say to her mama if that happened? How would you square yourself with her pa? Goddamn if I ain't got a mind to bust you one myself. Now you take her home and don't let me see you around here no more. As for *you*"—turning to the silent and trembling girl—"all I got to say is you better get yourself a better beau. Such damn fools as this one is poison to a religious young lady, and don't you go telling me that ain't what you are. *I know, I* do. Now, scat, the goddamn bothen of you!"

Whereupon he half bowed and half heaved them onto the waiting trolley car, and stood by muttering until it started back to the city.

From all this the maker of snap judgments may conclude that Julius was a Puritan at heart—perhaps even that there was a Y.M.C.A. secretary hidden in him. Nothing could be more untrue. He simply did not want to clutter up his conscience, such as it was, with gratuitous and unnecessary burdens. Otherwise he was the complete antinomian, and of all the tough and abandoned trolley parks around the periphery of Baltimore, his Sunset was undoubtedly the worst. Every sort of infamy that the vice crusaders of the time denounced, from crap shooting to hoochie-koochie dancing, and from the smoking of cigarettes by females—then still *contra bonos mores*—to riotous boozing by both sexes, went on within its gates, and there was no dilution of these carnalities by anything of an even remotely respectable nature. If a customer had called for a lemonade the waiters would have fanned him with the billies they carried up their sleeves, and if either of the two comedians in the so-called burlesque show that went on in a big shed had ventured upon a really clean joke, Julius himself would have given him the bum's rush. The striptease had not been invented in that remote era, but everything that the fancy of ribald men had yet concocted was offered. The stock company, like most other such organizations, played a loutish version of *Krausmeyer's Alley* every night, but it was given with variations suggested by the worst conceits of whiskey drummers and medical students. The taste of the time being for large and billowy women, there was no girl in the chorus who weighed less than 170 pounds, and the rear elevation of each and every one of them was covered with bruises from head to foot, all made by the slapsticks of the comedians. In the intervals of the performance on the stage, these ladies were expected to fraternize with the customers. This fraternizing consisted mainly in getting them as drunk as possible, and then turning them over to scamps who dragged them out to a dark spot behind the shed and there went through their pockets. When a customer resisted—which happened sometimes in the case of sailors—the scamps gave him a drubbing, and it was not at all unheard of for the harbor cops to find the clay of a jolly jack-tar in the adjacent river, especially of a Sunday morning, for Saturday night was the big night at Sunset Park, as it was at all such places.

The land cops, who knew Julius when he was a poor flatfoot like themselves and now took a certain amount of fraternal pride in his success in life, made occasional raids upon him, but only under pressure from reformers, and never with any hope or intent of bringing him to heel. Once I was present when a party of reformers undertook a raid in person, with a squad of cops trailing along, theoretically to protect them. Julius, who was on watch as usual at his front gate, let them enter unmolested, but they had hardly snooped their first snoop before his whole company of goons, male and female, fell upon them, and in two minutes they were in full retreat, with the cops following after to clout them as they ran. The next day he swore out a warrant for their leader, charging him with lifting a diamond sunburst worth $18,000 from one of the chorus girls, and under cover of the ensuing uproar their countercharges were forgotten. Julius had a dozen witnesses willing to swear that they had seen the reformer throttle the girl with one hand and grab the sunburst with the other, and another dozen schooled to testify that they had recovered it only by *force majeure* and in the face of

---

And He Didn't Rise Too Well Afterwards Either   The legendary 19th-century champion drinker of Würzburger beer was Baron Ferdinand Sinzig. One evening in New York City in 1889, the Baron drank thirty-six seidelsfull of Würzburger at one sitting. It is said that he didn't rise once during the feat.

---

wild slashings with a razor by the accused. The sunburst itself was brought into court, along with five cut-rate jewelers hired to certify to its value, and for a while things looked dark for the poor reformer, for he was a Sunday-school superintendent, and Maryland juries, in those days, always said "Guilty" to Sunday-school superintendents; but his lawyer filed a demurrer on some obscure ground or other.

Rather curiously, there was seldom any serious disorder at Sunset Park—that is, within Julius' definition of the term. Now and then, to be sure, a sailor ran amok and attempted to stage an imitation of some massacre he had seen in Shanghai or Port Said, but he seldom got beyond teeing off, for all of Julius' waiters, as I have said, were armed with billies, and his head bartender, Jack Jamieson, was a retired heavyweight, and worth a thousand men. Even the comedians in his show lent a hand when necessary, and so did the four musicians who constituted the orchestra—the leader, Professor Kleinschmidt, who doubled on piano and violin and fed the comedians; the cornet player, George Mullally; the trombonist, Billy Wilson; and the drummer, Bing-Bing Thompson, himself a reformed sailor. Julius himself never entered these hurly-burlies, but stood on the sidelines to boss his lieges. Even when a customer insulted one of the lady help, say by pasting her in the nose or biting off an ear, the head of the establishment restrained his natural indignation, and let the *lex situs* prevailing at Sunset Park take its course. Only once, indeed, did I ever hear of him forgetting himself, and on that occasion I happened to be present as his guest, for he was always very polite to newspaper reporters, as he was to detectives, precinct leaders, coroners and other such civic functionaries.

It was the opening night of his 1901 season, and I made the uncomfortable trolley trip to the park in the company of Leopold Bortsch, *Totsäufer* of the Scharnhorst Brewery, who had to attend *ex officio*, for Julius had Scharnhorst beer on tap. Unfortunately, there had been complaints about it of late, as there had been in Baltimore proper, for it was then, and had been for years, the worst malt liquor ever seen in the town. Leopold himself, who had to drink it day in and day out on his tours of customers' saloons, and at the innumerable funerals, weddings, wedding anniversaries, christenings and confirmations that went on in their families, was constrained to admit, in candid moments, that it was certainly doing his kidneys no good. But when a Class A customer had an opening, he had to get it down willy-nilly, and at the same time he had to foment its consumption by all the assembled bibuli. For the first night of Sunset Park, which in a normal week consumed two hundred half barrels, he was expected to stage a really royal show, and to that end the brewery allowed him $100 to spend over the bar. He did not know, as he marched up radiating his best promotional manner, that there was trouble ahead. Specifically, he did not know that Julius, succumbing at last to the endless complaints about Scharnhorst beer (which had by now become so bad that even the Scotch engineers from British ships sometimes gagged at it), had resolved to give a look-in to seven other Baltimore breweries. Nor did he know that all of their seven brews were already on tap at the bar, and that he would find the *Totsäufer* of each and every one lined up before it, to fight him to the death.

It was a shock, indeed, but Leopold was not one to be easily flabbergasted, and his reply was characteristically prompt and bold. The immemorial custom was for a *Totsäufer* to begin proceedings, on such an occasion, by slapping down a five-dollar bill and inviting all comers to have a beer. Leopold slapped down a *ten*-spot. The seven other *Totsäufer*, thus challenged, had to respond in kind, and they did so with panicky dispatch, each, of course, calling for his own beer. Jack Jamieson, for the opening night, had put in two extra bartenders, which, with his regular aides and himself, made five in all, but how could five men, within the space of five minutes, draw 1600 five-cent glasses of beer? It seemed beyond human power, but I saw them do it, and while they were still shoving over the last couple of hundred—by now at least 80 percent foam—Leopold threw down *two* ten-spots, and commanded a double ration of Scharnhorst for all hands. What would the other *Totsäufer* do now? What they would do was instantly apparent. Six of the seven saw him with crisp *twenties*, and simultaneously bellowed orders for wholesale rounds of their own beers. The seventh, Hugo Blauvogel of the Peerless Brewery, raised by peeling off *three* tens.

The situation, as the war correspondents say, now began to develop rapidly. Jack Jamieson relieved it somewhat by palming one of the twenties and one of the tens, and his chief assistant helped a little more by collaring another of the tens, but there remained the sum of $130 for the cash register, and a simple calculation will show that it called for 2600 beers. Half of them had been drawn—God knows how!—before Jack thought of raising the price to ten cents, but by that time the bar was packed as tightly as a busload of war workers, and great gangs of reinforcements were swarming in from all parts of the park. When the news reached the hoochie-koochie show, where a hundred or more sailors from the Battleship (*censored*), then on a goodwill tour of the Atlantic ports, were spoofing the performers, they arose as one man, and began a lumbering sprint for the bar. Passing the show-shed on their way, they gave the word to its patrons, and in ten seconds the girls and comedians were mauling and jawing one another to empty tables. Not a waiter was left on the floor, and in half a minute more not a girl or comedian was left on the stage, or a musician in the orchestra pit. By the time these artists arrived at the bar the crowd in front of it was twenty-men deep, and all semblance of decorum had vanished. The boozers close up were so dreadfully squeezed and shoved that they could hardly get down the beers in front of them, and the later-comers on the outskirts fought in despair for better places. The sailors from the battleship, forgetting chivalry, tried to climb in over the heads of the ladies of the ensemble, and the comedians, musicians and special

"The way I figure it, the law of averages is on our side . . ."

policemen slugged it out with the waiters. Only the eight *Totsäufer* kept their heads. They went on throwing money into the whirlpool of suds that covered the bar.

Up to this time Julius himself had been at his usual post at the park gate, searching the faces of inpouring fair ones for vestiges of innocence. But he had ears as well as eyes, and though it was a good city block from where he stood to the bar, he eventually picked up the roar that was mounting there, and made off to investigate. The crowd, by now, bulged outside the entrance like a swarm of flies around the bung of a molasses barrel, and hundreds of newcomers were arriving at a gallop and trying to horn and worm their way into it. Julius accordingly ducked to the rear, and entered behind the bar. He was just in time to hear Leopold Bortsch give the signal for the final catastrophe. It consisted of the one word "Wine!" uttered in a kind of scream. "Wine! Wine! Wine!" echoed the massed and macerated boozers. "He's opening wine! He's setting up wine! Hooray! Hooray! Hooray!"

There were, in fact, but five bottles of wine in the whole of Sunset Park, and they had been lying in Jack's cooler for three or four years, awaiting the remote chance that John W. Gates, Stanford White or Charlie Schwab might drop around some evening. The first two were duds, but the remaining three popped with magnificent effect, and as the so-called champagne seethed out of them, the last restraints of civilized society blew off, and the whole company yielded to its *libido boozalis*. In half a minute not a single sailor from the battleship was on the floor: they were all climbing over the merchant mariners and other civilians, and in dozens of cases a sailor thus climbing had another sailor climbing over *him*. Julius, with his long experience as cop and *Wirt*, saw a riot was in the making. "No more!" he roared. "Not another goddamn drink! The bar is closed!"

Alas, it was a bad idea, and even if it had been a good one it would have come too late to work. As well challenge Behemoth with a spit-blower or Vesuvius with a squirt. Jack and his colleagues, in obedience to the boss's command downed their tools instantly, but there were plenty of sailors present, both of the Navy and the Merchant Marine, who knew very well which end of a bottle had the cork, and they were over the bar in no time at all. Nor were they bound and hobbled, once they got into action, by the stiff, professional technique of Jack and company. When an outcry for gin came from the far reaches of the crowd they sent a whole bottle of it sailing through the air, and then another. Nor did they hesitate to use bottles on Julius' own head when he plunged into the thick of them, and essayed to lay them out. Of the details of this phase I can give you only hearsay, for I had been working my way out since the beginning of the action, and had by now taken a rather unfavorable post of observation some distance away, behind a large oak tree. But I went to the trouble during the weeks and months following to run down the full story, and these were its principal elements:

1. The rioters emptied not only every container of lawful goods in the park, from beer kegs to sprinklers of Angostura bitters; they also got down a barrel of cologne spirits that Julius used to sophisticate his five-cent whiskey, the contents of forty seltzer siphons, and a bottle of Mickey Finns.

There are two times when you can never tell what is going to happen. One is when a man takes his first drink; and the other is when a woman takes her latest.

—O'HENRY

2. Julius' first act, on recovering his faculties, was to get a revolver from his office and go gunning for the eight *Totsäufer.* All had disappeared save Hugo Blauvogel. At him Julius fired six times, missing him every time. The next day he served notice on the Baltimore breweries that any *Totsäufer* sent to the place thereafter would be shot like a dog.

3. The sailors from the Battleship (*censored*), returning aboard at dawn, took with them five of the ladies of the Sunset Park ensemble and both comedians. The officer of the deck refused admission to the ladies, but apparently swore in the comedians as mess attendants, yeomen, chaplain's mates or something of the sort, for a couple of weeks later the men of the whole North Atlantic Fleet staged a show at the Guantanamo base that is still remembered in the Navy as the damnedest ever seen. Its stars were two comics of unprecedented virtuosity. From the first glimpse of their red noses to the last reverberation of their slapsticks, they had the assemblage rolling in the aisles.

the three pigeons

by oliver goldsmith
(1728–1774)

LET schoolmasters puzzle their brain
  With grammar and nonsense and learning,
Good liquor, I stoutly maintain,
  Gives *genius* a better discerning.
Let them brag of their heathenish gods,
  Their Lethes, their Styxes and Stygians,
Their *qui's* and their *quae's* and their *quods*.
  They're all put a parcel of pigeons!
    Toroddle, toroddle, toroll!

When Methodist preachers come down,
  A-preaching that drinking is sinful,
I'll wager the rascals a crown
  They always preach best with a skinful.
But when you come down with your pence
  For a slice of their scurvy religion,
I'll leave it to all men of sense,
  But you, my good friend, are the pigeon.
    Toroddle, toroddle, toroll!

Then, come, put the jorum about,
  And let us be merry and clever,
Our hearts and our liquors are stout,
  Here's the Three Jolly Pigeons for ever!
Let some cry up woodcock or hare,
  Your bustards, your ducks, and your widgeons,
But of all the gay birds in the air,
  Here's a health to the Three Jolly Pigeons!
    Toroddle, toroddle, toroll!

Books are not the only things that can fill a library. Listen to Roy Andries de Groot tell you about his collection of very short stories on colored glass.

And then let him show you how to replace your Ping-Pong table with a much more entertaining cellar.

how to manage your liquid assets

by roy andries de groot

IF YOU enjoy the classic pleasure of drinking wine with your dinner and want to develop your understanding so that you can present the proper wines to your guests, it is essential to set up some sort of storage arrangement even if you live in an 18th-floor apartment and open only two or three bottles a week. There is no magic about an underground cellar.

Recently, when I spent a few days at Château Latour, the wine master took me for a tour of the cellars. After walking, it seemed, for miles among barrels and racks of bottles, he opened a side door and we stepped out into full sunshine. If Château Latour does not need an underground cellar, I certainly do not! In fact, I would just as soon call it my "wine library." I choose my bottles as carefully as my books and stack them as neatly on rack-shelves, so that any bottle can be found and pulled out within two or three seconds.

50 BOTTLES IN FOUR PARTS

I divide my wine library among four areas in my New York apartment. I use the simplest type of wooden, eight-bottle rack in the kitchen, at the farthest possible point from the heat of the stove and sunlight of the window. Here, I keep two or three bottles of strong, peasanty reds and richly aromatic whites, always in half-bottles so that they are quickly used up. Also, I have strong kitchen versions of Port, Sherry, vermouth, which, because they are fortified, keep easily. Finally, there are some Cognacs, Armagnacs and California brandies for adding zest to many dishes, for marinating fruits and for flaming.

128   THE BOOZE BOOK

"If you haven't tried it lady, don't knock it!"

The second division of my wine library is a mobile, 12-bottle
stainless steel rack on wheels, which is normally kept within reach of
my dining table, but can be moved around to any strategic spot for a
party. Here, I store my least expensive wines for everyday use—
bottles to be opened for a family supper, for a glass with my
luncheon tray at my desk or for the instant slaking of a sudden thirst.

The third and main part of my wine library is a honey-combed
"wine wall," facing away from the light in an air-conditioned room
where the temperature is never allowed to rise above 68°F. or fall
below 50°F. I deliberately store these party wines at from 10° to 15°F.
above the normally accepted temperatures in order to age and
develop them slightly more quickly for use within the year. This wall
is made up of single-bottle, aluminum or plastic cells clipped
together to cover any shape or size of available wall space. It is
entirely flexible. It can be dismantled at the drop of a hat and its units

reshaped to fit into any other space. It can be made to hold 50 bottles—or 50 hundred.

The fourth, most glamorous division of my wine library is a locked closet, kept always at a temperature of around 50°F., where the noblest wines I can afford are left to age gracefully. They represent, shall we say, a liquid capital reserve—a savings account of rare and special pleasures and, as with savings in a bank, they increase steadily in value.

EQUIPMENT AND CONSTRUCTION

If you are an amateur carpenter you can, of course, simply turn to one of those excellent little books filled with plans and diagrams. Since I am not the wood-working type, I have used the various standard racks of metal, plastic or wood that are available in virtually every size from six bottles to 600 and at prices that start at about 50 cents per bottle. This means that the least expensive type of wooden rack reinforced with steel rods (which I use in my kitchen) costs, for the eight-bottle size, around $4.

This single-bottle calculation is the best scale by which to judge the value of wine racks when shopping around. I believe they should be purely functional. But, naturally, if you allow yourself to become dazzled by fancy designs, you can pay an arm and a leg. One rack of sexily curving plexiglass holds 30 bottles and costs $150, or $5 per bottle. There is also a 24-bottle refrigerated closet at $400, or almost $17 per bottle.

The single-bottle honeycomb cells for my wine wall, in plastic or aluminum, cost between $1.50 and $3 per bottle and are probably the most flexible of all wall systems. In my locked closet, where I age nobler wines, I have lined the walls with the most inexpensive form of storage rack I have ever been able to find: ten-inch lengths of standard four-inch diameter, fired-clay drainpipe—the kind used in the building industry. Since they are reasonably heavy and solid, they stack, row upon row, into a strong unit with no attachments or cementing required. Also, because the clay is a reasonably good heat insulator, they resist sudden variations in temperature and thus protect the valuable bottles. The last time I bought some of these clay pipes, they were selling at around 35 cents for each one-bottle piece.

What to do if you have no cellar or closet capable of being separately air-conditioned for precise humidity and temperature control? The answer is one of the new California redwood "Wine Vaults," custom-built, locked, individually air-conditioned, walk-in closets, which store the wines in darkness and with humidity control at a constant temperature of around 55°F. They come in different sizes to hold a minimum of 132 bottles at an average cost of $7.20 per bottle, up to a maximum storage of 1824 bottles at an average cost of $1.80 per bottle. Another advantage of this type of unit, of course, is that it can be taken apart and moved with the furniture from one home to another.

HOW TO RATE WINE

There are three essential things you should do every time you pull the cork of a bottle that is new to you. (And, of course, you should always buy a single bottle before you buy a single case.) With the first sip, you should rate the wine on a scale of from 1 to 20—with 10 being the median average for a wine that seems to have no troublesome faults and no particularly noticeable virtues. With the second sip, you should relate the quality score to the price, to produce a value rating. If the bottle, for example, rates 12 quality points and costs $12, then its value rating is a dollar per point. This system enables you to compare the values of all wines at all prices. I

 Let us eat and drink; for tomorrow we shall die.

—ISA. 22:13

assure you, from long personal experience, that you will be amazed by the results. Third—and most important of all—you should feed your ratings, together with the basic facts from the labels, the prices, and your comments, into a small, simple card file.

As soon as you have, say, the first 20 wines carded, you will have a ready-made shopping list for future purchases. If you also note down on the cards the foods that were successfully served with each wine, your card file becomes a personal, menu-planning guide. Always remember that your taste buds have a poor memory. Even one week from today you will not be able to recall accurately your judgments. Developing a card filing system makes you the master of your wine destiny.

THE CHOICE OF WINES

It is just as ridiculous for one wine lover to tell another exactly what he should have in his cellar as it would be for one book lover to set up the library for a friend. It is a matter of personal taste. One man's Côtes du Rhône is another man's Inferno. You can, of course, start a wine library with three bottles or 13, but I think that a more flexible and practical beginning would be half a dozen bottles for cooking, half a dozen inexpensive labels for everyday drinking, two dozen medium-priced for party meals and one dozen rather more expensive bottles to lay down for the future. This makes a starting total of 48—a nice, round figure, so easy to halve or quarter, or to double or quadruple, according to your ambition. As to what your first inventory should be, all that your *Tastevins confrères* can do is to offer a few expressions of personal opinion.

American wine connoisseurs seem to me to be strangely different from their *confrères* in other wine-growing countries. A Frenchman would hardly ever dream of drinking anything but the vinous products of his homeland. Italians drink their own wines. Spaniards drink theirs. So do Portuguese, Greeks, Luxembourgers, Yugoslavs, Hungarians, Australians, Chileans, Mexicans, Canadians and all the others. Only Americans seem to be different. Here connoisseurs are still so much imbued with the snobbish conventional wisdom of a hundred years ago, which assumed that prestige and quality resided exclusively in French and German labels, that they have for years shamefully underestimated their own American wines.

At this point in the argument, I have always in the past felt obligated to say that when it comes to the dozen or so supreme wines of France and Germany we have not yet developed individual

---

Claret is the liquor for boys, port for men; but he who aspires to be a hero must drink brandy.

—BOSWELL's *Life of Dr. Johnson*

---

vineyards of completely matching status. But such has been the speed of progress in the last few years in wine technology that even this statement can now be largely and seriously challenged. We have individual vintners in California of extraordinary skill and dedication and, as they have available more and more of the older vines essential to the production of the aromatic grapes that make the great wines, they are producing more and more vintages of incomparable quality.

SOME OF THE BEST BUYS

In recent months, I have tasted bottles of red California Cabernet Sauvignon which, in side-by-side comparisons, were several points better than some of the finest chateau-bottlings from Bordeaux. At another tasting, three magnificent labels of white California Pinot Chardonnay, again compared side-by-side with their European counterparts, were rated several points ahead of even a great Le Montrachet from the Côte d'Or of Burgundy—the wine that has been acclaimed for centuries as the greatest white in the world. (Incidentally, at this moment of writing, the average cost of these supreme American Pinot Chardonnays is under $10 per bottle, while the French Le Montrachet is over $25.)

When it comes to the medium-priced and inexpensive wines, where you can begin to discount the costs of transatlantic shipment, import duties, the devalued dollar, etc., our home-grown wines in terms of value for each quality point, are virtually beyond competition.

The basic reasons are immediately obvious to any professional in the wine business. The high-quality, estate-bottled wines of France and Germany are tightly limited to a fixed and unexpandable supply. The law forbids the enlargement by even one square foot of the registered vineyard of Chateâu Lafite, or of any other of the so-called *appellation contrôlée* vineyards. The supply is fixed, against a continually rising world demand.

There is no such limitation in American vineyards. Whether it is in New York, or Ohio, or Michigan, or in the new Yakima Valley vineyards of Washington, the rising demand is being met by an immense expansion of vineyard plantings. In California, for example, there are now almost 150,000 acres of wine-producing vines. But, in addition to this, almost 100,000 new acres have been planted in noble vines, so that they will gradually come into production over the next five years.

How does all this affect the stocking of a new wine cellar? My own solution to the problem has been, over the past couple of years, to explore, to taste and to rate every available American wine, to compare them directly with their imported counterparts and to fit the best American labels into the practical patterns of my wine library.

THE FIRST 50 BOTTLES

This list must be flexible since these wines are not always available. However, equivalent values can be found in any well-stocked wine shop.

Begin with a single mixed case of tasting bottles to explore your own preferences.

Three light, dry, everyday wines:

1. A 1971 Alsatian Sylvaner from one of the famous makers such as Dopff, Hugel, Trimbach, etc., at about $3.25.
2. A 1972 Muscadet from the Sevre-et-Maine district of the Loire by Barré Frères at about $3.25.
3. A California Chenin Blanc from Almaden, Chapellet, the Christian Brothers, Inglenook or Krug at about $2.25.

Three rich or sparkling whites for party dishes of fish or light meats:

4. A fine 1969 or 1970 district label from Chassagne or Puligny-Montrachet in Burgundy at about $5.
5. A noble California Pinot Chardonnay from Beaulieu, Freemark Abbey, Masson, Mondavi or Stony Hill at about $5.
6. The charming sparkling Seyssel Blanc de Blancs, Le Duc, from the mountain vineyards of the Savoy, an extraordinary value at about $5.50.

One sweet dessert wine:

7. A 1971 regional French Sauternes from Johnston of Bordeaux at about $5.75.

Three light, fruity reds:

8. A fine 1970 or 1971 regional Côtes du Rhône from the vineyards around the village of Beaumes-de-Venise. Many of these labels represent excellent value at around $2.50.
9. A 1969 or 1970 California Zinfandel from Martini, Mirassou or Wente at about $2.50.
10. A 1969 or 1970 Bordeaux vineyard bottling of a less well-known label such as Ch. Loudenne, Ch. Simard or Ch. La Vieille-France at about $4.50.

Two richly aromatic reds which will improve with keeping:

11. A 1967 Chianti Classico like a Riserva from Nozzole, an above-average value at about $4.25
12. A noble 1969 Chapelle-Chambertin from Clair-Daü in Burgundy at about $8.50.
13–24. Your second case essentially could be a repetition of the first to expand your stock—and your knowledge, by enlarging your experience of the wines you liked.

"No, I don't want to arm-wrestle to see who buys the next round!"

For the next 16 bottles, you might buy four each of some of the most versatile wines:

25–28. Four bottles of the light, white 1960 Crépy from Fichard at about $3 each.

29–32. Four bottles of the 1970 Tavel rosé from the Ch. d'Aqueria of the Rhône, about $4.40 each.

33–36. Four bottles of a fine, light California Grignolino from Beringer, Heitz or San Martin at about $2.75 each.

37–40. Four bottles of the dark, dominant, rich 1970 Cahors from the Lot valley in southwestern France—an historic wine now available for the first time here—about $3.75 each.

Finally, ten bottles which are noble now, but will probably be great in another ten years:

41. The 1969 Ch. Haut-Marbuzet from the Médoc in Bordeaux at about $4.75.

42. The 1969 Ch. Labégorce from Margaux in Bordeaux, about $5.

43. The 1970 Ch. Monbousquet from St. Émilion in Bordeaux at about $3.20.

44. The 1969 Ch. Pontac-Monplaisir from Graves in Bordeaux at about $4.

45. The 1970 Bon Theurons from Burgundy at about $8.75.

46. The 1970 Clos Vougeot from Guyot in Burgundy at about $9.

47. The 1969 Grands échézeaux from Mongeard-Mugneret in Burgundy at about $10.40.
48–50. Three more bottles of the 1969 Chapelle-Chambertin, as in the first case, at $8.50 each.

Total—$230.70

When Irving Berlin wrote Moonshine Lullaby, *James Villas found a national anthem.*

Collecting coins and baseball cards are fine enough hobbies, of course, but here's a new one that will make every boy on the block want to trade with you.

i made my own wine

by james villas

FELLOW connoisseurs of the grape: Have you ever even thought about making your own wine? No? Well, unless your next of kin just happens to be a Rothschild, Lichine, or Schoonmaker, or unless you know a few friendly buyers or someone connected with a chic wine society, you might do well to give the idea some consideration if you have any intention of stocking your cellar for the future. And the reasons should be obvious enough.

Just a few years back most of us could afford cases of superb Beaujolais and California wines, a reasonable number of bottles of first- and second-growth Bordeaux, and, for special occasions, perhaps a ceremonial La Tâche, Corton, or magnum of Dom Pérignon. But now even the most reckless oenophiles gasp in disbelief when given a chance to study the inflated prices quoted monthly in *Beverage Media*, the Bible of the wine-and-spirits industry. As the American appetite for wine continues to grow, buyers and speculators on today's conglomerate market have not only been grabbing up every bottle of good wine available (both foreign and domestic) but also pushing prices to absolutely incredible heights.

So what's the solution? The most logical idea (and one that might bring those in the industry back to their senses) would be to give up wine altogether and begin drinking Pepsi again with dinner. Unfortunately my own passion for wine has remained too overwhelming for me to resort to this primary type of gustatory prostitution, but at least I made some effort to test out a few secondary types.

First there was the rosé binge, then I struggled through a jug-wine phase, and next I learned about "special natural wines" (or, if you prefer, "mod" or "pop" wines) selling at one dollar a bottle and accounting for twenty percent of the nation's wine consumption. All failed.

Convinced the possibilities of ever again having decent wine at a price I could easily afford were exhausted, one of my more astute fellow drinkers casually suggested I try making my own. A brilliant, exciting idea which sounded simple enough and which sent unimaginative me scurrying off with hope for my parched palate. If the English had been producing inexpensive but excellent homemade wines for decades, why shouldn't I give it a try? God knows, I had no more vinaceous integrity to lose!

Almost everybody has at least heard about the wine-making kits presently being marketed throughout the country, but at first I wasn't about to succumb to such amateurism. No indeed. I fully intended to attempt a top-notch professional job, buy and stomp my own grapes, learn about yeasts, etc. (After all, I was no dummy in chem class and I did learn about Pasteur's theory that when yeast attacks the natural sugar of grape juice, carbon dioxide is gradually released and after a while you have vino. All very basic.) Then I began reading about the importance of hydrometers, vinometers, acid-testing kits, sterilizing equipment, and clarifying agents, all of which sounded not only pretty complicated but also dreadfully expensive. What really brought me to my knees, though, was a short

 It's Also Not Bad in the Shade   A man hath no better thing under the sun than to eat and to drink and to be merry.

—ECCLES. 8:15

article I began studying pertaining to fermentation. Now be honest, would you too not have chickened out when confronted with something like this mess:

"The 3-phosphoglycerate is converted to pyruvate which, in turn, is converted to acetaldehyde. As the acetaldehyde is formed, it becomes a hydrogen acceptor and through enzymic conversion produces the ethanol. This process dominates the rest of the fermentation."

I'd had enough. So began the hassle of choosing what appeared to be the best kit of those widely available on the market. I finally chose one designed to enable epicures to produce five gallons (twenty-five bottles) of Burgundy "equal to the best Europe has to offer at a mere fraction of the cost," and it arrived at my small brownstone apartment exactly three days after it was ordered. The all-inclusive price: $19.95. The parcel, no larger than a hatbox, contained, according to the enclosed booklet, the following unbelievable number of items: 1. three quart cans of gourmet-quality super-concentrated (Spanish) grape juice; 2. five-gallon (plastic) fermentation container; 3. bored stopper; 4. (plastic) fermentation air lock; 5. nontoxic (plastic) siphon tubing; 6. wine yeast; 7. wine-yeast nutrient; 8. citric acid; 9. soluble campden (sterilizing) tablets; 10. wine stabilizing tablets; 11. wine-bottle labels and corks. Everything necessary for twenty-five bottles of wine except tap water, five pounds of sugar, and the bottles.

After perusing all the weird-looking packets and gadgets, I turned to the step-by-step instructions of the booklet, concocted as directed a quart of sterilizing fluid in an empty cranberry-juice jar (my preferred therapeutic beverage, by the way, for a glutted liver), and began the lung-boggling feat of blowing up the inflatable fermentation container until it assumed the shape of a mammoth plastic jug. Totally exhausted, I had to rest before carefully washing, sterilizing, and rinsing every piece of preliminary equipment I saw in the box. (Make note of that important last verb; you'll understand why in a minute.)

Following the directions word for word, I made marks six inches and ten inches up from the bottom of the container, left my well-lighted working area in the kitchenette for my poorly lighted bathroom, stepped inside the bathtub, and proceeded to fill the jug with warm water to the six-inch mark. Back in the kitchenette, I funneled five pounds of white granulated sugar into the container (really about four pounds, twelve ounces, since I got bored and twice over-poured), screwed the cap on, and shook as vigorously and laboriously as I would a two-pound whiskey sour.

After spending a quarter of an hour searching for a church key (that archaic tool which still has its unique value in these twist-off times), I removed the three cans of grape juice from pots of hot water in which the concentrate had been loosening, punched two holes in each top, tasted the glop, gagged, spilled a few indelible drops on my shirt and into the sink, and emptied the cans rather awkwardly into the container. Next the packets of yeast, yeast nutrient (a compound that allegedly gives the yeast an extra kick), and citric acid, then more shaking, then another haul back to the bathtub to fill my plastic incubator to the ten-inch mark. The booklet finally directed that you must once more "invert the fermentation container several times to make sure all the ingredients are mixed." Well, I would defy even a gorilla to try to "invert" what I dragged over the side of the

"Phoebe, we were supposed to have the sitter home by midnight!"

tub! I found the one and only way to wrestle with the weight of that mother was to lie back flat on the floor, roll the flabby container up onto my midsection, clasp it in my arms, and exercise obscene body contortions. The technique worked.

Once I got the container safely balanced on top of a high stool in an appropriately dark area of my hallway, I read that I was to remove the cap, insert the tubular capped air lock in the bored stopper, pour a little water and sterilizing fluid into the network of tubes, fix the apparatus tightly into the neck of the container, and . . .

Bored stopper? Panic! I didn't remember sterilizing *any* type of stopper or cork with a hole! A thorough search of the kit, the kitchenette, the drain in the sink, the tub, under chairs—everywhere and no bored stopper! Absolutely certain that this essential item had been left out of the kit and that rapid primary (or aerobic) fermentation (the action of which could be properly checked only by observing the speed with which the water moved in the air lock) was already beginning, I had to improvise fast by substituting for the plug a wet rag wrapped around the base of the air lock and crammed as tightly as possible in the neck. It worked, I guess, for, sure enough, the water began going up one tube and down the other.

Afterward I shot to the phone, made contact with the distributor who admitted "such mishaps do occur in packing," and was assured of receiving the bored stopper in one day. It arrived in four, and in the meantime all havoc had broken loose inside that jug. Weird sounds, huge purple bubbles climbing up the sides as oxygen escaped the onslaught of growing yeast, and my entire apartment smelled as if someone had sprayed it with a grape-scented aerosol.

Since I was honestly trying to make my wine in strict accordance with the directions (no matter how simplistic, vague, and, above all, non-explanatory they were), I was thrilled when the envelope containing the bored stopper finally arrived. Thrilled, that is, until I discovered that the stopper was made of hard plastic and that it wouldn't fit into the neck of the container. Now, believe me, you have never experienced real frustration until you've tried to cut, file, burn, even chisel hard plastic! Knives, razor blades, steel files—you name it, I tried it, and only after going out and buying a pair of authentic surgical scissors did I succeed in crudely reducing the size of that plug. Of course, each time I removed my well-functioning rag contraption to see if the stopper would fit, fresh air (the great enemy of wine) was gushing into the container and the water in the air lock was moving slower and slower. I still don't know how important all this was (very, I should suspect), but by the time I got the

---

Give wine unto those that be of heavy hearts.

—PROV. 31:6

---

hacked-up stopper in place and sealed the miserable object inside the neck with black masking tape, the aqueous life inside the air lock was practically nonexistent. Still, I retained hope that my wine would survive this ludicrous ordeal.

From the moment primary fermentation began till the day—nine weeks later—I siphoned the wine into bottles, just about every procedure required a good deal of imagination and even greater guesswork. What do you do, for example, when the instructions state that the ideal atmosphere should be 65 degress Farhenheit and the controlled room temperature of your apartment rarely drops below seventy-five during the summer? Easy. You change the location of your window air-conditioner, turn all the vents in the direction of the container, keep the unit running full blast day and night, wear a light sweater, and steady yourself when the electric bill arrives. Of course if you made wine in winter and your apartment had a thermostat, your only problem would be the risk of catching

---

 Two Fingers of Wrigley's Please   The ancient Greeks preserved their wines with the gum of pine trees. After many years of such drinking, they came to believe that wine was supposed to taste this way.

---

pneumonia. If there were no thermostat (as in my case), you would simply keep opening and closing all the windows, never invite guests in, and risk catching an even worse case of pneumonia.

The most irritating of all guesswork throughout the process pertained to interpreting the timing directions. How would you react to such vagaries as: "After about eight to fourteen days [do so and so]," or (now get this!) "After about four to eight weeks the fermentation should have ceased"? Half by newly acquired instincts, half by a self-invented system of logistics, I eventually learned to approximate the timing of various steps, filling the container with cold water to an indicated level on the tenth day, waiting the necessary nine (not four, not eight!) weeks for the secondary fermentation without air to cease (proof: no bubbles), etc. From beginning to end I kept a daily chart, making notations on the brew's colorations, odors and scum; the water level in the air lock; and when and why I thought (i.e., prayed) the yeast was converting the sugar into alcohol and all that nasty CO_2 was being released. I became more and more fascinated with my living creation, bought more books on wine, read extensively, and would catch myself gawking at the container for a quarter of an hour several times a day, waiting for a bubble to move or pop or mysteriously fade out of sight.

When, after all those pregnant weeks, the concoction displayed no more bubbles or foam, out came the plastic siphon and into boiling water went corks and all the Sprite, Pepsi, and used wine bottles I'd been collecting. As you might have guessed by now, I'm something less than adept at anything mechanical, so it'll come as no surprise that when I began sterilizing all those bottles in two large roasting pans (still another feature on which the booklet offered no suggestions), I scalded practically every inch of my body not protected by clothing. But it was too late in the game to allow anything like aching flesh to stand in the way of success, so I bravely smeared my pitiful arms with Solarcaine, rushed out and bought a very expensive pair of asbestos gloves, picked up my corncob tongs again, and proceeded to sterilize each and every cork and bottle.

Since the booklet warned against disturbing whatever sediment might have accumulated in the bottom of the container, I got my friendly neighbor (whose name I swear I still don't know and who asked no questions) to help carefully move big baby and stool from the hallway to the kitchenette. Just as I was about to remove the air lock, I noticed for the first time a tiny speck on top of one tube. Figuring it was no more than a morsel of sediment that had somehow worked its way up into the air lock, I didn't pay it much attention and continued taking out the appartus. Then, holding the air lock to the light, I became a little more apprehensive and decided to pour the water into my hand to study the foreign object more closely. I touched it, fiddled with it a bit, and . . . No! It couldn't be! But, by God, it was, because it started to move by itself! Yes, a bug! A detestable reddish bug which after I pounded it dead, displayed two detestable little wings. Now don't ask me where it came from, its genus, how it sneaked down into the capped air lock, or how it survived on top of the water. I don't know and don't want to know and would appreciate not being informed about the disgusting creature. Let's just forget about it.

I was never taught as a youngster to siphon gas from automobiles, but I quickly learned the gravitative principle behind the art while filling my wine bottles. Naturally there were a few initial disasters. Wine spewing in my eyes and all over the floor, permanently stained clothing, and mouthfuls of filthy sediment when I allowed the siphon to drop too near the bottom of the container. But in the long run I perfected the skill, checked each tube full to make sure the wine was clear (and bugless!), and tightly corked enough bottles of Burgundy to serve an army. The work was finished. No doubt there had been obstacles, but I'd managed to overcome most and must say I felt the pride of a Burgundian while racking my wine to age in the bottles. Naturally I was anxious to properly taste what I had produced, but, as I said, I did want to give the kit every fair chance and sneaking a taste of the raw wine would have gone against all the rules.

The booklet stated that my gourmet wine could be drunk as shortly as three to four weeks after siphoning. Although I must admit I found the notion rather shocking, I took the company's word and decided to conduct a wine tasting exactly one month after corking. I bought a loaf of French-style bread, a package of imported crisp *biscottes*, and three different varieties of beautifully ripened cheese. I set out my finest crystal goblets, one large, clear decanter plus a stack of pads on which my very closest of friends could record their reactions. Don't get me wrong. I did have faith—I was determined to have faith—in my thirteen-week-old homemade Burgundy, but my better instincts told me that I would be smart to invite only those honest souls who love me and who, even at the risk of being poisoned, would see me through any crisis.

The moment came. I had uncorked the wine thirty minutes before the tasting, a few people snickered at the Pepsi bottle, but everyone observed carefully as I poured the Burgundy into the decanter. The color did look a little dark, but we could detect no sediment and, thanks be, I saw no bugs. I filled each glass halfway. We swirled, snifted the bouquet, then sipped. No reaction from anyone. More swirling, snifting, sipping, then some began making notes. Intolerable silence, interrupted only by a few Ummm's and Ug's and tongue lappings like a dog trying to reach food stuck to his nose.

At first my prejudiced brain convinced me the wine was drinkable, but soon my palate asserted its power, assuring me that what I was sloshing around in my mouth should best be described as a very light grape-flavored Communion wine with a touch of gasoline. I kept

---

At Least It Wasn't Draino   Napoleon carried cognac on all his campaigns, but it was primarily for sanitation.

---

quiet. My friends, grabbing for the cheese and bread like dying slaves, tried to be polite—although I did notice they'd quit writing on their pads.

One said the wine was "interesting," another "like nothing I've ever tasted before," while another asked if she could go to the bathroom to cleanse her palate before tasting again. Finally, after thirty minutes of torture, my oldest and dearest and most respected sybarite placed his glass firmly on the table, looked at me in somewhat of a daze, and candidly announced, "It tastes like absolute hell!"

I was crushed, although I knew he was right. Of course I was still stubbornly certain that the reason the wine was so dreadful was because it had not had sufficient time to mature in the racks. But what if, after a year or so, it was still glop? Besides all the time and effort I'd spent producing the equivalent of twenty-five bottles, how much, importantly enough, had it all cost me? The best I could figure, if what I had to shell out for sugar, telephone and electric bills, masking tape, a Magic Marker, scissors, gloves, a chisel, Solarcaine, three new shirts, bread, and cheese were added to the $19.95 charge for the kit, the total would run to exactly $129.61, or $5.18 per bottle. For that amount, if I purchased by the case immediately, I could probably have stocked up for the next year on plenty of my favorite '72 Moulin-à-Vent Jadot! On the other hand, there was a principle and a lot of pride involved, and who could say, as the booklet had encouraged, someday I might have found my Burgundy to be one of my most treasured assets.

I didn't have much time to contemplate the alternatives, for within a day or so after the tasting my candid friend sent me a clipping from a back issue of *Playboy* that literally made my knees buckle. Some fellow loner had written to whomever you write at that magazine to inquire about some law governing bachelors making their own wine. The researched response was as follows:

"Federal law states that the head of a household may produce for 'food value and medicinal purposes' up to 200 gallons of wine a year without paying taxes on it. He must file Form 1541 with the Bureau of Alcohol, Tobacco and Firearms to get his exemption. Most bachelors do not qualify as heads of households. Unless you have a legal dependent living with you, you may not make wine tax-free."

I staggered in utter shock and disbelief. There couldn't possibly be such an archaic law! But I checked further and, indeed, it's all true; no person or booklet had informed me of this insanity; I had broken the law and the I.R.S. had every right to march into my apartment and confiscate all my Burgundy and maybe even throw me in jail.

Well, that was the final blow. Within minutes I was dumping the contents of each and every bottle of my potentially valuable vinaceous asset into the toilet, and, with wrath in my soul, I now challenge any federal inspector to find a trace of homemade wine in my apartment. Most of you are in the lucky position to take up legally what is becoming a very popular and tax-free hobby. I can't promise you'll have successful results, but at least you're free to try. Unfortunately, my wine-making days are over—that is unless my dog develops a demonstrable passion and medically proven need for Burgundy and qualifies as a legal dependent on Form 1541.

The man who rhapsodizes about port at the front of this book here widens his scope to include the entire world of drink, which he surveys with insight and charm.

"We are content to stand or fall by the congeniality of our drinking habits," says this imbibing Baedeker, who now will tell you, among countless other things, why the English like their beer warm and the Danes like their schnapps ice cold.

modus bibendi

by alec waugh

"WILL SOMEONE take me to a pub?" So ran the refrain of one of G. K. Chesterton's happiest ballades. I have often quoted it to myself when the Madame Secretary of a lecture club has displayed for my admiration the cultural and civic ornaments of the community whose elite I am to address that afternoon. The library, the swimming pool, the oratorium, the cathedral, the park are potent proofs, no doubt, of a high standard of industry and social consciousness, but I should get a clearer insight into her fellow citizens if she would take me to a saloon and I could observe how they relaxed.

A nation reveals itself in its drinking habits. The various airlines —American, Asian, European—vie with one another in their advertisements to explain what is that "little something," that treasured secret that makes them different from and superior to all other lines. I have flown by most of them, and they are all the same; identical in service and routine, with the quality of the meals and comfort determined by the class you travel—first, tourist or economy. In one respect only have I found any difference among them: the kinds of drinks they serve and the way in which they serve them. In no other way, if I were taken onto an aircraft blindfolded, could I guess under which flag I flew.

A trim, brisk hostess is at your elbow with an order list. "Would you like anything to drink before your lunch? Beer, gin and tonic, sherry?" Britain is taking care of you. A small tumbler is put upon your table, a trolley is wheeled down the aisle. "Cinzano, Dubonnet, St. Raphael?" Where else but in France could you be? A highly salted herring canapé bites your palate, a small cold glass smelling of aniseed is set before you. Ah, Scandinavia! There is the rattle of ice on aluminum. "Martini or manhattan, sir?" This is the U.S.A. The invariable "delicious, complimentary meal" will follow, but you have your map reference.

We are the products of our soil and climates—mentally, emotionally and socially; our natures are determined by the degree of latitude on which we live; so are our drinking habits, which are the expressions of those natures. There are basic differences among the Latins who are wine producers, the English and Germans who are beer producers, and the northerners—the Scandinavians, the Scots, the North Americans—who hit back against the cold with spirits. Wine drinkers as a general rule drink during meals; whereas the advocates of beer and spirits drink before and after meals. The sidewalk cafés of France and Italy are expressive of a wine drinker's way of life, just as the Third Avenue saloon fulfills the demands of the man who escapes shivering from Arctic cold, throws quickly upon his stomach a short sharp shot of fire, then as warmth revives him looks round for company among other orphans of the storm.

Between the beer drinkers of Germany and England there is a difference imposed by climate. The German summer is very hot; its winter is very cold and its rooms are appropriately heated. England, the beneficiary as she is the victim of the Gulf Stream, is neither frozen in winter nor baked in summer. Central heat is for the most part a superfluity, and tropical-weight clothes are rarely needed.

 Two Great Minds That Were Moist   Confucius said that he was sometimes "overcome by wine," a thought you don't find on too many fortune cookies.
  And Socrates said, "So far as drinking is concerned, you have my hearty approval, for wine does moisten the soul and lull our griefs to sleep."

Clammy is the definitive epithet, and English draft beer is an admirable antidote to that. Indeed, only in England could it be drunk at all. It is flat and tepid and American GIs were very properly warned against it when they crossed the ocean. But in England it is rarely hot enough for one to need cold beer. On the few occasions when it is, tepid beer can be exceedingly unpleasant, particularly during austere periods of rationing when the brew is denied its fair share of malt. I remember returning to England from America in the summer of 1948. It happened to be a torrid day. There was a cricket match at Lord's and I went straight to it. I was thirsty. I ordered a half pint of bitter; its lukewarm bouquet was redolent of chaff and dust; only the dignity of my surroundings prevented me from spitting it upon the floor. But on a winter's day, seated before a fire, in a taproom, there is little better than a tankard of draft beer that has been cooled but not chilled in a publican's cellar; nor is there anything much better on a bland August evening, under an apple tree, in a garden. Anyhow, it suits England.

The difference between the English and Germans is illustrated not only by the taste of their different beers but by the atmospheres within their inns. The Germans are intensely musical; they also like being organized; they relish athletic rallies and massed parades. The English are competitive individualists. Where the Germans sit round a table, emptying steins and singing songs, the English enjoy quiet games like darts, shove ha'penny and dominoes. The atmosphere of a German beer garden is faithfully reproduced in the East 80s in New York, and an extremely cosy atmosphere it is, too. In January 1939, feeling certain that war was imminent, I returned to Europe from New York by a German ship, the Hansa, long since sunk. I wanted to remind myself before the curtain fell of how many pleasant things there were in Germany. One evening there was a Bavarian party, with the crew dressed in the national costume. It was very gay; it was hard to believe that within seven months friendship between a German and a Briton would have become impossible.

But it must not be forgotten that Germany is even more famous for its wines than for its beers; we make a mistake in thinking of Germany exclusively in terms of its beer gardens. There is the *Weinstube*, too, those dark little rooms, with a grape sign hanging over the door, where in the twilight of a paneled peace you sip cool, clean wine out of long-stemmed glasses. For close now on a century, the world has been distraught by the contrast between what we love and what we hate in Germany; would it be too fanciful to suggest that all we cherish most in Germany, her poetry, her music, her philosophy, spring from the *Weinstube* and that the noise, the regimentation, the ostentation spring from the beer garden, dearly though, at its best, we love it? The beer garden and the *Weinstube*— is there a conflict there? Perhaps that is stretching an argument too far. But is any country more divided within itself than Germany, and does any country present two such different ways of drinking?

In France there is no equivalent for the *Weinstube*; the French take wine with their meals and they take their meals at home. It is a general custom for a man to go home to lunch. There was no restaurant in Paris before 1765; and restaurants did not begin to

"We first met in a bar not far from here, when Mr. Armitage sent a note to my table with one of the waiters. It wasn't much of a note, really, but how much can you write on a hundred-dollar bill?"

flourish until the revolution made the supply of servants scanty. The sidewalk café, a result of the introduction of coffee into France in the middle of the 17th Century, was essentially a place where you drank coffee. Until then, France had only known the *auberge*, the traveler's inn. Coffee appealed to the French temperament, but Louis was distrustful of the café; he feared it as a center of sedition, just as Charles II across the Channel, in spite of Catherine of Braganza's addiction to tea, regarded the coffeehouse with suspicion.

Both the café and the coffeehouse survived their monarchs' strictures and their separate fates are indicative of the difference between France and England. The sidewalk café has retained its pristine character. The French go to cafés before and after meals; to drink coffee and eat a pastry in the afternoon, to sip an aperitif before dinner, to take a cordial with their coffee after dinner. The

---

Drink today, and drown all sorrow.
You shall perhaps not do't tomorrow.

—JOHN FLETCHER

---

café became an extension of the home, or rather, an alternative to the home. The Frenchman's home is a moated fortress; it is easier for a stranger to gain admittance into a Turkish harem. Without the café, life would be very dreary for the Frenchman; he must have somewhere to sit and watch life drift by. Socially, in the 19th Century it developed into an ancillary of the *salon*, each café having its own clientele, each café becoming the center of its own political and esthetic creeds. George Moore, arriving in Paris in the 1880s, found his university, his education—emotional and artistic—in the Place Pigalle, in the Nouvelle Athènes; the young American today finds his equivalent in Montparnasse, in La Rotonde and Les Deux Magots.

The fate of the coffeehouse in England was very different. The Englishman's home may be his castle, but its doors stand open. While the English inn has always attempted to be a home from home, the London coffeehouses became clubs, White's and Brooks' and Boodle's, where far less coffee was drunk than port and brandy, where cards were played for extravagantly high stakes—and did not Max Beerbohm write in his essay *A Club in Ruins*, "It had been more than a home; it had been a refuge against many homes; it had been a club"?

The English pub, on the other hand, has retained its pristine character as a home from home. The history of the English pub is indeed the history of England. It was not until the dissolution of the monasteries that inns spread over England—although it was from an inn that Chaucer's pilgrims set off for Canterbury. Before Henry VIII's quarrel with the Pope, country inns were not needed; travelers put up in monasteries. But under Elizabeth, road travelers needed safety and comfort for the night. Monarchy was concerned that the inn should retain that essential status, and not become a shelter for the spread of dangerous, heretical ideas. Charles II enjoined in his *Tippling Act* that the inn should be "a place for the receit, relief, lodging of wayfaring people; it is not meant for the entertaining and harboring of lewd and idle people to spend and consume their time and money in lewd and idle manner." But the inn survived, fulfilling an essential need of the English character.

The urban pub, in particular the London pub, has become a microcosm of English life, which logically combines democracy with class distinctions. We, Britons, are all subjects and equal under the Crown, but we recognize differences between ourselves, differences that are exemplified by the English pub. In a Public House there are three bars—in order of status, public, private and saloon—catering to men and women of different income groups and different social standing. The prices and amenities are different. You enter by separate doors, but the wooden divisions between the bars do not reach the ceiling; the same roof is over all and the publican and his staff move without hindrance round the inner circle from one bar to the next.

The architectural heyday of the pub came in the middle of the 19th Century. The Victorian gin palace, with its efflorescence of applied ornament, its elaborate brass rails with their triple gas burners, the decorated plate glass softening the glare, the embossed wallpaper, the Corinthian capitals, the rich mahogany was for the slum dwellers of the day what the movie palaces were to be to a later generation. The "home from home" had become grander than anybody's home. In a higher degree than ever before the heavy swells of the day could, under the incrusted ceiling, preserve their anonymity—the small half-opened windows, pivoting on vertical axes, the mahogany framework of the saloon bar protecting the perpendicular drinker from impertinent scrutiny.

The old English inn was essentially an alehouse; and that it has remained, in spite of the changes that have been forced upon English habits by the caprices of their rulers' foreign policies. During the 14th and 15th centuries England owned Aquitaine, and the noble wines of Bordeaux flowed onto English tables. Then there was a change toward the sweet heavy fortified wines of Spain and of Madeira, which proved an effective antidote to the chill, damp climate. The age of port began when William of Orange's hatred of Louis XIV of France encouraged him to place exorbitant taxes on French wines and spirits and lower the tariff on wines from Portugal. But beer has always been the national drink in England.

It was beer for the most part that the American GI drank during his exile across the water, and in spite of its unexpected taste most ex-GIs, when they return with their families to England, make straight for the nearest village inn. More than one of them on his return from the wars, when asked about the English, replied, "There can't be anything too wrong with a country that has an institution like the village pub." It is the answer that most Englishmen would soonest hear; a Frenchman would equally like to hear it made about the sidewalk café and a German about the *Weinstube* and the beer garden. We are content to stand or fall by the congeniality of our drinking habits.

The foreign countries that I have loitered in are as vivid in my memory for their drinking habits as for their landscape, architecture, climate, ways of dress. I recall Martinique as much for its rum punches as for its green and towering mountains, over one of which there always seems to be a rainbow curving, and for the long flowing dresses of its womenfolk, the scarf over the shoulder, the handkerchief knotted into the hair in points. Rum is the staple drink of the West Indies; every punch is made on the classic formula "one of sour, two of sweet, three of strong and four of weak," but the basic taste of each island's rum is different. My personal belief in the superiority of Martinique rum is founded on the fact that its punches are prepared more simply, require less sophistication, than those of any other island except Barbados. In Fort-de-France, you sit at a rickety wooden table in the shade, looking out across the savanna to the white statue of Josephine, with its sentinel royal palms; you order a punch, specifying that you want old not white rum; a waitress will set before you a bottle of rum, a couple of limes, a glass of syrup, a red-brown earthenware pitcher that has cooled, through evaporation, the water it contains. You mix your punch yourself, by the classic formula; the lime, the syrup, the rum, the water. Two punches sipped slowly send you to lunch in an anapaestic mood. Whenever I travel in a French ship, I order a rum punch at noon. The flavor of that rich, sweet, powerful liquid carries me back to Martinique.

Japan is the country of formal courtesies. On my first day in

Tokyo, I asked the director of the British Council against the committal of which solecisms, which breaches of etiquette, I should be most on my guard. He replied, after deliberation, "Never be impatient, never be angry. Impatience and bad temper are things which the Japanese do not understand." The drinking habits of the Japanese confirm this excellent advice. To most tourists, possibly, the traditional tea ceremony serves as a symbol of the country's way of life. It is certainly elaborate and picturesque, but it is lengthy, and I found the thick green fluid that I was eventually invited to sip most unpalatable. I felt about the tea ceremony in Japan much as I felt about the kava ceremony in Fiji.

That, too, is an experience no visitor should miss. I doubt if any male, other than a Fijian, could be stimulated physically by a Fijian belle. Her shoulders are broad, her ankles thick, her features heavy and her black hair sticks up on end as though it had been trained by a topiarist. Yet when she is arrayed for the kava ceremony, in bright clothes with her face painted, she does not have the bizarre attraction of a Mardi Gras grotesque. And the ceremony itself is not unimpressive, with the chief dipping something that looks like hemp into a bowl of water and wringing it out into another bowl which he proffers with formal courtesy to his guests. But the brew itself has a dirty, gritty taste; moreover, it is completely unalcoholic. The Fijians themselves find it as invigorating as the English housewife does her morning cup of tea, but I suspect that the lack of warmth I felt for the people of Fiji was the result of my inability to appreciate their kava.

Pure water is the best of gifts that man to man can bring,
But who am I that I should have the best of anything?
Let princes revel at the pump, let peers with ponds make free;
Whiskey or wine or even beer is good enough for me.

—ANON.

Indeed, had Japan had nothing more invigorating than its tea ceremony to offer, I am very sure that I should not have returned there within 13 months. Mercifully it had a great deal more to offer: its sake and its geishas.

The Japanese are experts at manufacturing articles that resemble their American and European originals. They produce whiskey and champagne that look as though they had come from the Highlands and from Épernay, and which if used in moderation have no deleterious effects. But the hot rice wine, sake, is the true *vin du*

"A double martini and a bag of peanuts, please."

pays. The small white-and-blue decanters in which it is presented and the small shallow white-and-blue cups out of which it is sipped are in accordance with the customs of its people. Sake is very light. It is not a distilled spirit. You can drink a great deal with impunity. A glass holds very little. This allows the ritual of innumerable refillings to be performed without trepidation. I attended my first geisha party in Osaka. I was warned before it began that on no account must I fill my own glass myself; though I might refill those of my hosts and fellow guests. I was also warned that before I drank I must raise my cup to whomsoever had filled it for me. For several hours a number of elegant creatures attended to my needs. The final memories of a geisha party are, or should be, vague, but I know that I felt well next morning, and I still carry in my luggage the small white-and-blue sake cup to remind me of the happy hours I spent in Tokyo, Kyoto and Osaka.

There is a kinship between the drinking habits of the Japanese and Danes, though no two drinks could be less alike than aquavit and sake. My memories of Copenhagen are very warm. I spent the whole of a recent winter there. Hotels are empty then, but though January and February are not tourist months, for Copenhageners that is "the season," when the ballet and opera are in residence and the court is at Amalienborg. There are no friendlier people than the Danes. In London, New York and Nice, I manage to half lose my temper three or four times a week; someone or something contrives to irritate me, but after I had been a month in Denmark I realized that I had not lost my temper once. It was not that I had become gentler-natured, but that the lighthearted tempo of Danish life precluded irritation.

In some ways the Danes are a formal people. There are certain courtesies that you must not neglect. You should never arrive as a guest without flowers in your hand or without having sent flowers earlier in the day. And when you next meet your host and hostess, you must not forget to thank them for their hospitality almost before you have said anything else, charming and gracious rules that it is well to absorb young till they become second nature. Equally gracious are their drinking customs. Beer and schnapps are the country's produce. Schnapps is taken at the beginning of the meal with a highly flavored hors d'oeuvre, raw herring preferably. It is very strong, so strong that it must be drunk ice cold. Two small glasses will suffice. You must never drink schnapps unless you are toasting someone or being toasted, but you must never toast your hostess; injudicious or ill-intentioned guests might force her to drink more than she might consider prudent. The toasting in schnapps is a half stage in gallantry; you raise the glass; your eyes meet a lady's; you smile and you say "Skoal!"; you sip; then, as you lower your glass, your eyes again meet hers in a smile. Every newcomer to Copenhagen is given a lesson in the ritual of drinking schnapps. For me the heart of Denmark is in that ritual.

If one is out of sympathy with the drinking habits of a country, one is unlikely to feel in tune with it. Fiji was an unlucky place for me not only because of the kava ceremony. Hospitably though I was cherished during my three weeks in Suva, persistently though I was taken round the clubs and round the bars, by the end of the third day I was beginning to wonder why I had met so few women; in club after club I had found males, young and elderly and old, standing coatless at a bar, pouring cold beer down their gullets. I inquired if there was a dearth of marriageable females on the island. No, no, I

A Yangtze Groucho Marx   The ancient Chinese poet, Li Po, wrote:

*The rapture of drinking
And wine's dizzy joy
No man who is sober deserves.*

---

was assured; most of the men, even the youngest ones, were married. Times had changed in the islands. Malaria had been stamped out; phrases like the white man's exile and the white man's grave applied no longer. Air conditioning and air transport had solved a hundred problems. Men married young and brought their wines out with them.

"Where are those wives?" I asked.

"At home; cooking, looking after the children."

"Don't they ever come here?"

"Not often."

I was puzzled for a little, then I understood. Fiji is administered by the British Colonial office in Whitehall, but its white population is mainly from Australia and New Zealand, and the custom of "the hour's swill" had been imported. It is a custom unique to Australia. Bars open early there, at 10:30. They remain open through the afternoon, but they shut at six. Males, therefore, when their offices close at five, go straight to their favorite bar and, standing shoulder to shoulder, gulp cold beer that has a nine-percent alcoholic content, hastening the pace and volume of consumption as six o'clock approaches. They then stagger out into the cool evening air. In New South Wales the custom has recently been modified and bars reopen at 7:15, so that a wife has been given a sporting chance of getting her claws into her husband's shoulder.

No one is certain whether this regulation was imposed out of deference to the puritans, the publicans or the politicians. The puritans for obvious reasons; the publicans because of the cost of labor, the reluctance to run a second shift; the politicians because they wanted to get the manual laborer to work on time and fit next morning. The hour's swill is, for the uninitiated, an intimidating experience. It is something that he should not miss; but its transportation, even in a modified form, even as a corollary, did not heighten my enjoyment of Fiji. I should have preferred more females at the bars and fewer males.

I spent two thirds of World War II in the Middle East—in Egypt, in Lebanon, in far Baghdad, mostly among Moslems, to whom the use of alcohol is forbidden. But in Lebanon, Moslems and Christians alike drink arrack. Arrack is a generic label. The Lebanese variety is distilled from grapes; it is white with a tinge of blue; it clouds when you pour water on it. It tastes of aniseed—it was in Beirut that I acquired a taste for Pernod. An insidious drink, it was forbidden to troops during the war, and Arab street vendors made high profits out of the sale of spiked oranges, into which arrack had been injected. If you do not eat while you are drinking arrack, you become quickly drunk; that is where its danger lies. It must be handled with circumspection. Moreover, it leaves a coating of powder round the stomach. You may wake in the morning after an arrack evening, thinking yourself recovered but feeling thirsty. You gulp a tumblerful of water and you are drunk again. The water has mixed disastrously with the powder, on an empty stomach.

Arrack demands leisurely drinking. There lies its charm. In cafés it is served with mezé, four or five dishes of hors d'oeuvres, olives, cheese, ham, radishes. At an arrack evening with a Lebanese family, you will spend three or four hours consuming four or five glasses of arrack, with fresh dishes of hot appetizers, sausages, cheeses, small birds, being presented every half hour or so. More than once, at an arrack evening, I have been too interested in the conversation to eat enough. At Western cocktail parties, out of regard for my weight, I am careful to ration my consumption of pre-prandial canapés. In Beirut, chattering away, lifting my glass periodically, I have become suddenly and alarmingly aware of the ceiling revolving to meet the floor. But a couple of quick mouthfuls of food have restored my equilibrium.

The tempo of arrack sipping is in admirable accord with the leisurely tempo of the Levant. Lebanon has been for many years a

French sphere of influence; the vine has been tended carefully and many sound pleasant wines have been produced there, but for me arrack is the key to the country. I spent a congenial winter and early spring there in 1942, and it was a happy day for me in 1950 when I landed early on a May morning at the Damascus airport and drove across the Bekáa valley to Beirut. I was surprised at first and disconcerted by the number of new buildings that I saw around me; would I find it very changed, too changed? Then in an unredeemed slum area, acrid upon my nostrils, came the stale smell of last night's arrack. My heart exulted; I was home again.

From Lebanon in 1942 I crossed the desert to Baghdad. Engaged there in counterespionage, one of my chief problems was my ignorance of the Arab way of life. I needed to understand the kind of man whose activities I was watching. Speaking no Arabic, I resorted to a familiar practice. Wearing civilian clothes, I would sit in an Arab café, watching over the top of my newspaper, the hooded Moslems, who would sit motionless for hours, upright in their hard rectangular wooden settles, sipping at their coffee; alone or silent for the greater part, but when they talked elaborating what they had to say with graceful, evocative, deliberate gestures. Dignified, impassive, unhurried, they appeared to be utterly detached from the radio that blared above their heads and from the traffic of the street outside; but the movements of their hands suggested mastery, power, firmness when they did resort to action. The men who were names to me upon a file became less strange, less foreign when I was back in my office reading an agent's report on them.

Whenever I go to a new country, one of my first requests to the friend or guide who is showing me the sights has been, "Please take me to the equivalent of an English pub." How I wish that in the days when I was a publisher I had commissioned an anthropologist to compile a study of the world's drinking habits. What a valuable book it would have been; what a pleasant assignment, too, for him. How he would have enjoyed his research. Now and again you run into a fight in a bar, but for the most part human beings are at their best there. Did not a poet say—

> Whoe'er has travell'd life's dull
> round,
> Where'er his stages may have been,
> May sigh to think he still has found
> His warmest welcome at an inn.

But is that a cause for sighing? And need the round be so dull, if there is an inn to round it off?

song from
"the school for scandal"

by richard brinsley sheridan

(1751–1816)

HERE'S to the maiden of bashful fifteen;
    Here's to the widow of fifty;
    Here's to the flaunting extravagant quean,
And here's to the housewife that's thrifty.

    Chorus.   Let the toast pass—
        Drink to the lass,
    I'll warrant she'll prove an excuse for a glass.

Here's to the charmer whose dimples we prize;
    Now to the maid who has none, sir;
Here's to the girl with a pair of blue eyes,
    And here's to the nymph with but one, sir.

    Chorus.   Let the toast pass—
        Drink to the lass,
    I'll warrant she'll prove an excuse for a glass.

Here's to the maid with a bosom of snow;
    Now to her that's as brown as a berry;
Here's to the wife with a face full of woe,
    And now to the damsel that's merry.

    Chorus.   Let the toast pass—
        Drink to the lass,
    I'll warrant she'll prove an excuse for a glass.

For let 'em be clumsy, or let 'em be slim,
    Young or ancient, I care not a feather;
So fill a pint bumper quite up to the brim,
So fill up your glasses, nay, fill to the brim,
    And let us e'en toast them together.

        Chorus.   Let the toast pass—
                Drink to the lass,
        I'll warrant she'll prove an excuse for a glass.

Remember the repeal that Robert Benchley talked about? Well, here's a splendid account of what was repealed, a vivid portrait of a boozeless New York. You'll especially enjoy reading about the security system in the old Club 21, a James Bond setup that made whiskey self-destruct.

how prohibition failed in new york

by john kobler

> After one year from ratification of this article the manufacture, sale or transportation of intoxicating liquors within, the importation thereof into, or the exportation thereof from the United States and all territory subject to the jurisdiction thereof for beverage purposes is hereby prohibited.
> —The Constitution of the United States of America, Amendment XVIII

THE DATE was January 16, 1920, a Friday.

"At one minute past twelve tomorrow morning a new nation will be born. . . . Tonight John Barleycorn makes his last will and testament. Now for an era of clear thinking and clean living!" proclaimed the Anti-Saloon League of New York.

For administrative purposes, the country had been divided into ten departments, each headed by an assistant commissioner. In addition, each state had a federal prohibition director with an assistant and a legal adviser. At the lowest echelon, confidently poised for action, stood 1,500 recently invested, gun-toting revenue agents. Immigration and Customs officers, plus tens of thousands of state, county, and city police, completed prohibition's army. "The penalties for violation are so drastic," trumpeted New York's chief revenue agent, Colonel Daniel Porter, "that the people of New York will not attempt to violate it. There will be no violations to speak of."

A federal judge's last-minute decision sowed panic among the legion of tipplers who had been piling up reserves in warehouses and safe-deposit vaults against the coming of the great drought. Private hoards so stored, the judge ruled, would be liable to seizure after midnight of January 16; home would be the only inviolable depository. All day, all over the country, chaos reigned as the frantic hoarders commandeered everything on wheels they could find to convey their liquid treasure from condemned shelters to domestic sanctuary. Booze-laden flivvers, limousines, vans, horse-and-buggies snarled street traffic, while pedestrians struggling with luggage, go-carts, baby carriages and receptacles of every description turned the sidewalks into obstacle courses.

The popular urban pleasure palaces observed the death of the old era with a mixture of resignation, melancholy, and forced gaiety. In New York City, where heavy snow was falling and the thermometer read 18 degrees, mock obsequies marked the approach of midnight. Tom Healey, the owner of the Golden Blades Restaurant, a resort renowned for its ice-skating extravaganzas, had a coffin paraded around the dance floor for everybody to throw his last bottle and glass into. Louis Fischer, who ran Reisenweber's café, had sent black-bordered cards to his regular clientele, bidding them to a funeral ball. The ladies who accepted received vanity cases in the shape of coffins. At midnight, six waiter-pallbearers carried a real coffin across the room to the strains of Chopin's "Funeral March."

Not all imbibers accepted their loss meekly. When a Brooklynite named Kiren Leishin entered his favorite saloon minutes after midnight and was refused a drink, he laid about him with a club, inflicting severe damage upon glassware, bottles, and the proprietor.

In "Satan's Seat," as prohibitionist Bishop Cannon referred to New York City, Congressman Fiorello La Guardia, an embattled wet, predicted at the outset of the Noble Experiment: "In order to

Now's the time for drinking.

—HORACE

enforce prohibition it will require a police force of 250,000 men and a force of 250,000 men to police the police." By 1922, about 5,000 speakeasies dotted the metropolis, and a few years later Police Commissioner Grover A. Whalen, with his glistening top hat and gardenia boutonniere, was estimating the number at 32,000, or more than twice as many as the legal drinking spots existing before prohibition. Congressman William P. Sirovich put the total closer to 100,000.

Variety, the bible of the entertainment world, frequently pub-

"Give them a couple of drinks, put out some salted nuts
and hope they don't stay for dinner."

lished the fluctuating prices of liquor as charged at selected speak-easies or other retail sources. Before prohibition, the average New York saloon price of a highball or cocktail, containing one ounce of liquor, ran two for a quarter, straight whiskey 10 to 15 cents a shot, and beer a nickel a schooner. With prohibition, prices doubled, tripled and quadrupled, but supplies were so plentiful and competition among bootleggers grew so fierce that prices eventually dropped back.

The city's reputedly wettest street was 52nd between Fifth and Sixth Avenues, and while it is apocryphal that liquor could be bought in any building there, certainly nobody had to take many steps along the brownstone-lined thoroughfare to slake a thirst. Robert Benchley once counted 38 speakeasies on 52nd Street. Such was the street's reputation that a lady who occupied a guiltless brownstone between two speakeasies was obliged to post a sign: THIS IS A PRIVATE RESIDENCE. DO NOT RING. Among the more renowned neighborhood oases were Tony's, favored by magazine editors, writers and illustrators, whose owner, Tony Soma, practiced yoga and sang operatic arias while standing on his head; razzle-dazzle Leon & Eddie's, with its entrance sign, THROUGH THESE PORTALS THE MOST BEAUTIFUL GIRLS IN THE WORLD PASS OUT, and Eddie Davis, a former carnival wheel-man turned singer, convulsing the clientele with such ribaldry as "She Came Rolling Down the Mountain" and "Virgin Sturgeon"; the Town Casino Club, glorying in a neon-lit, electrically operated fountain that sprayed a nude naiad with jets of multicolored water; Janet of France, a theatrical rendezvous and the only speakeasy (according to its proud *patronne*, Janet Martire) ever visited by the abstemious George Bernard Shaw; Jack & Charlie's or Club 21 (after its address, 21 West Fifty-second Street), perhaps New York's farthest-famed speakeasy, a status it achieved largely through the early patronage of Benchley, Dorothy Parker and Alexander Woollcott. To shield its habitués from the prying eyes of newspaper columnists, the co-founders, John Karl Kriendler and Charles Berns, allowed none to cross the threshold. In an effort to generate snob appeal, they were also known to turn away, or relegate to back tables, persons they deemed insufficiently ornamental.

The late Charlie Berns remembered 21's elaborate security system: "We had this engineer we trusted, and he installed a series of contraptions for us that worked on different mechanical or electrical impulses. For example, the shelves behind the bar rested on tongue blocks. In case of a raid, the bartender could press a button that released the blocks, letting the shelves fall backwards and dropping the bottles down a chute. As they fell, they hit against angle irons projecting from the sides of the chute, and smashed. At the bottom were rocks and a pile of sand through which the liquor seeped, leaving not a drop of evidence. In addition, when the button was pressed, an alarm bell went off, warning everybody to drink up fast. We had only one serious raid. The agents searched the building for 24 hours. They never found a single contraption.

"The most important was the secret door to our wine cellar." [Here Berns led the author down to the subterranean depths of the building. We paused before an alcove, its white walls bare, and he produced a long, thin steel rod.] "Unless you know exactly where to look, all you can see are solid walls, no visible cracks of any kind. But there's this tiny aperture here. You'd have to have an eagle eye." [He shoved the rod through.] "When I push this a little further in, you'll hear a noise. That's the tongue lock being released on the other side. It takes very little pressure on my part, even though with

---

The discovery of a wine is of greater moment than the discovery of a constellation. The universe is too full of stars.

—BRILLAT-SAVARIN

---

the steel-frame support the thing weighs over a ton. It works like a trigger on a gun. This is the only entrance or exit. No other way in or out. If the mechanism broke, we'd have to dig through the concrete and pull out the whole lock. But that never happened. And no agent ever discovered the cache either."

The majority of the city's smartest, highest-priced speakeasies, many of them owned or controlled by gangsters, clustered within a radius of half a mile from Rockefeller Center. On 58th Street, the suave ex-bootlegger, Sherman Billingsley, who introduced at his first Stork Club the predinner bowl of celery, olives, radishes and scallions buried in crushed ice, gave his patrons silk neckties emblazoned with a stork, and their ladies, perfume. In her 54th Street nightclub, Helen Morgan drew rivers of tears from her clientele as, perched upon a piano, she sobbed, "He's just my Bill." Two blocks north, at the Merry-Go-Round, Paris-gowned women and their dinner-jacketed escorts bestrode wooden horses as they sipped cocktails, while a circular bar revolved to the music of an electric organ. Zito, the Daumier of the speakeasies, had adorned the walls with caricatures of the better-known customers, like Lily Pons, Vincent Astor, Dudley Field Malone and Maurice Chevalier.

"Er . . . perhaps you didn't know, but we deliver . . ."

Merely to set foot inside Belle Livingstone's five-story Country Club on East 58th Street cost $5. Well advanced in years when she inaugurated what she described as "a salon of culture, wit and bonhomie," Belle, the ex-wife of a Chicago paint salesman, an Italian count, a Cleveland millionaire, and an English engineer, friend of European royalty and American tycoons, customarily wore Chinese red lounging pajamas and, being husky, personally ejected customers who failed to meet her standards of decorum.

The main salon of the Country Club, which had a capacity of 400, was decorated in Louis Quinze style. The upper floors offered such divertissements as Ping-Pong and miniature golf, available only to players who ordered drinks at frequent intervals. Prices started at $2 for whiskey and soda and peaked at $40 for a bottle of champagne.

Belle's only rival for the crown of Queen of the Speakeasies was Mary Louise "Texas" Guinan from Waco, a thrice-married former circus bronco rider, vaudevillian, and star of early two-reel Westerns, billed as "The Female Two-Gun Bill Hart." Less elegant, but as expensive as the Livingstone resort, Texas's El Fey Club at 107 West 45th Street, backed by the racketeer Larry Fay, netted $700,000 during its first year. Though El Fey featured a variety of bizarre entertainers, among them a girl calling herself Nerida, who danced with an eight-foot python twined about her nude torso, the stellar attraction was Texas herself, a calliope-voiced dyed blonde, sheathed in ermine and flashing a bracelet encrusted with almost 600 diamonds. Her *shtik* consisted of chaffing the customers. "Hello, suckers!" she would bellow at them as they entered, a greeting that became a catch phrase of the dry decade. "He's a good fellow!" she would exclaim, pointing to some blushing male sitting with his wife. "But for another woman." If the cash register failed to ring often enough, Texas would blow a whistle and raise her gravelly voice above the jazz band, and roar: "Come on, suckers, open up and spend some jack!"

At the opposite pole from these opulent playgrounds was a vast outcropping of dives in comparison with which the vilest of the old-time saloons seemed benign. The raw liquor they dispensed at best seared the throat, at worst blinded or killed the consumer. The "shock houses" of the Bowery and the Lower East Side did not hesitate to serve wood alcohol when their stocks of less noxious beverages ran low. During the single year of 1928, the poison killed more than 700 people in the Bowery alone.

Between these upper and nether extremes there evolved an agglomeration of modest, relatively decent saloons and cafés, selling drinks by the glass or bottle at no great risk to the customer's health or wallet. In addition, a variety of establishments, most of them originally unconnected with the liquor traffic, began carrying liquor as a sideline. Without too taxing a search, it became possible to find a drink on almost any block in the city. *The New York Telegram* once assigned a team of reporters to investigate the availability of liquor in the borough of Manhattan alone. They managed to buy it in "dancing academies, drugstores, delicatessens, cigar stores, confectionaries, soda fountains, behind partitions of shoeshine parlors, back rooms of barbershops, from hotel bellhops, from hotel headwaiters, from hotel day clerks, night clerks, in express offices, in motorcycle delivery agencies, paint stores, malt shops, cider *Stubes*, fruit stands, vegetable markets, groceries, smoke shops, athletic clubs, grillrooms, taverns, chophouses, importing firms, tearooms, moving-van companies, spaghetti houses, boarding houses, Republican clubs, Democratic clubs, laundries, social clubs, newspapermen's associations."

Bootleggers were omnipresent. One of them went so far as to scatter his handbills through the Federal Building, where, despite the assurances of New York's chief revenue agent, Colonel Daniel Porter, that nobody would be so foolhardy as to risk the drastic penalties imposed by the Volstead Act, an average of 50,000 alleged violators were arraigned every year. In 1925, the Department of Justice appointed Emory S. Buckner U.S. attorney for the Southern District of New York. The following year Buckner testified before a Senate subcommittee: "I found the fifth floor of the Federal Building a seething mob of bartenders, peddlers, waiters, bond runners,

And Then the Conference Moved *Under* the Table   According to Herodotus, the Persians never discussed important affairs of state unless they were feeling the influence of wine.

fixers. The air of corruption had even descended into the civil parts of the court, and reports were made . . . of attempts to bribe jurymen even in the toilets of the building."

In line with Section 2 of the Eighteenth Amendment ("The Congress and the several states shall have concurrent power to enforce this article by appropriate legislation"), most states enacted supplementary liquor laws. New York modeled its Mullan-Gage Law, adopted in April, 1921, on the Volstead Act. During the next three years the grand jury heard 6,904 cases. It dismissed 6,074. Of those that went to trial only twenty ended in convictions. Judge

Alfred J. Talley of the Court of General Sessions, who believed that as a result of prohibition, the United States had become "the most lawless country on the face of the earth," summoned the grand jurors to his chambers to ask them why they so rarely returned an indictment. The foreman explained: "The men tell me that they will not indict men for offenses which they are committing themselves."

New York, like most American cities, abounded in shops selling malt, hops, wort, yeast, bottles, crown caps, capping machines, rubber hosing, alcohol gauges and other paraphernalia for home brewing. Around these homely activities there grew up a major industry. Some economists believed that the sums expended for brewing materials, especially malt syrup, absorbed a large part of the average American household budget. In New York City alone, more than 500 malt and hops shops flourished, with almost 100,000 dispersed through the country, plus 25,000 outlets for assorted home-brewing apparatus.

In addition to the independent shops, the big food chains like Kroger Grocery, Piggly-Wiggly, and the A&P displayed great pyramids of malt syrup cans. The national production of malt syrup in 1926 and 1927 came close to 888 million pounds. Allowing a normal 10 per cent for nonbrewing uses, enough remained for 6.5 billion pints of beer.

The courts had ruled that there was nothing inherently illegal in any of these products—not unless specifically sold to make alcohol.

The end product of amateur brewing usually fell short of pre-prohibition standards. If the corks did not pop out or the bottles explode before their contents matured sufficiently to drink, you got a mud-brown liquid, smelling sourly of mash and tasting like laundry soap. As for the effect, one imbiber reported: "After I've had a couple of glasses I'm terribly sleepy. Sometimes my eyes don't seem to focus and my head aches. I'm not intoxicated, understand, merely feel as if I've been drawn through a knothole."

Section 29 of the Volstead Act, permitting the manufacture and possession of fruit juices for home consumption (under a later stipulation, up to 200 gallons per household), had been framed mainly to appease the farmer. But it proved a boon to viniculture. A California grape grower who killed himself, believing he faced ruin, could scarcely have imagined that during the next five years in his state alone grape acreage would expand sevenfold from 97,000 to 681,000 acres. Similar increases benefited the four other leading grape states—Michigan, Ohio, Pennsylvania and New York. The produce reached the customers as fresh grapes, or as bricks of Bacchus or grape juice, the last labeled, CAUTION: WILL FERMENT AND

TURN INTO WINE. From 1925 to 1929 Americans drank more than 678 million gallons of home-fermented wine, three times as much as all the domestic and imported wine they drank during the five years before prohibition. This figure did not include the wine made from backyard vineyards, from dandelions, currants, cherries and other fruits. Like home brew, winemaking stimulated the manufacture of related products—grape crushers, winepresses, fermenting tubes, gelatin to settle the sediments, crocks, kegs, bottles and corks—on which the home winemakers spent about $220-million a year.

Far simpler than brewing beer or fermenting wine at home was distilling alcohol. One primitive method called for nothing more than a little corn-sugar mash, a tea kettle, and a bath towel. The home distiller would heat the mash inside the kettle over a slow fire. Alcohol volatilizes at between 180 and 200 degrees Fahrenheit, and as the mash gave off its fumes, he would drape the towel over the kettle spout to absorb them. When he cooled the towel and wrung it out, it would yield a few drops of a vile-tasting but potent liquid. With patience, he could collect enough to jollify the whole household. Steam cookers, coffee percolators and wash boilers were also commonly used as receptacles for mash. But at a cost of only $5 or $6, the home distiller could buy the more sophisticated portable one-gallon copper still. For technical guidance he needed only to visit the public library, where he would find books and trade periodicals devoted to the subject. A series of *Farmer's Bulletins* published by the government between 1906 and 1910 would show him how to distill alcohol from fruits of all sorts, from grain, sugar beets, potato peelings. Once he had a batch of alcohol, he could quickly and simply simulate almost any desired type of liquor with additives. To produce a large quantity of gin, he would combine alcohol, water, glycerine and juniper oil in a bathtub. Because it was cheap and its taste readily disguised in cocktails, "bathtub gin" enjoyed considerable popularity during the early years of prohibition, as indicated by the sudden increase of juniper oil imports. Most juniper oil came from Italy and Austria and served little purpose outside of flavoring gin. An ounce sufficed to flavor several gallons. In 1920, almost 9,000 pints were imported; in 1925, almost 11,000.

By 1921, the one-gallon still had become a commonplace domestic utensil, and over some sections of the big cities the reek of sour mash hung like a miasma. "The worst crime a child can commit," said Will Rogers, "is to eat up the raisins that Dad brought home for fermenting purposes." The bloodthirsty, bootlegging Genna brothers of Chicago's "Little Italy" hired hundreds of its immigrant slum dwellers as "alky cookers" at $15 a day, installing stills in their kitchens and supplying them with the ingredients and operating directions. With only 178 agents to police more than a million New York homes, seizures were few.

Early on the morning of November 22, 1922, Jerry Costello, the owner of a Manhattan livery on East 107th Street, opened his door to two strangers, one squat, round and pursy, the other ponderous but considerably taller. They were, said the shorter man, speaking in a rich Italian accent, fruit and vegetable vendors. Their street cart had met with an accident, and they wanted to rent a horse and wagon for the day. While Costello busied himself hitching up a dray horse, the strangers wandered around the stable, eyes peeled and nostrils

And It's Ideal for Launching Dinghys Are you tired of good champagne and in the mood to make your own? Then take a fifth of dry white wine, a cup of brandy, and a quart of sparkling soda. Get them all as cold as possible and mix.

Maybe it won't be a Happy New Year salute, but it might warm up Ground Hog Day.

flared. At length they detected a winy aroma that drew them to a flight of steep, narrow stairs. With their bulk the descent was not easy, but they managed to squeeze themselves down into a basement storage room. There they counted 53 barrels of wine. "This is enough," whispered the shorter man, resuming the accents of their Lower East Side neighborhood. "You drive the wagon out a ways while I get a search warrant."

Izzy and Moe of the Prohibition Bureau had triumphed again. Hiding their cunning behind the mask of buffoonery, they had the appeal of funny-paper characters, and the press never wearied of reporting their antics. By an incredible diversity of dodges and disguises, they arrested, in the course of five years, almost 5,000 lawbreakers, the great majority of whom were convicted, and they confiscated more than 5 million bottles of booze worth about $15 million. Of all the prohibition cases prosecuted in New York City up to 1926, fully a fifth resulted from the wiles of Izzy and Moe.

Isidor Einstein was a 40-year-old, $40-a week postal clerk when the Volstead Act took effect. With a wife, four children and his father to support, he immediately applied for the slightly better-paid job of dry agent. Of Austrian origin, he spoke fluently not only German, but also Hungarian, Polish, and Yiddish; he also knew a little

Russian, Spanish, French, and Italian. In English, he could mimic any foreign accent.

Izzy's first target was a Brooklyn workingman's saloon. Wearing grease-stained overalls, he followed one of the habitués into the place, waddled up to the bar and ordered a near beer. Standing five feet five and weighing almost a quarter of a ton, bald, double-chinned and globular, he looked as harmless as a panda. "Wouldn't you like a lollipop on the side?" asked the barkeep acidly, causing merriment among the whiskey-drinking regulars. He was newly employed in New York, Izzy hastened to explain, and unfamilar with its customs, but lest he appear a piker, he would buy a pint of whiskey, if not too costly. The bartender sold him one, whereupon Izzy, in gentle, melancholy tones, pronounced the words that became his standard refrain: "There's sad news here. You're under arrest."

After a succession of coups, Izzy persuaded his old friend, Moe Smith, to join him in the service. Moe ran a cigar store on the Lower East Side and also managed a small boxing club, having himself fought professionally in his youth. A taciturn, introverted man, he was the perfect foil for the ebullient Izzy. Together they developed a repertoire of more than a hundred masquerades, not one of which, they claimed, their quarry ever penetrated.

The enforcement careers of Izzy and Moe ended abruptly. Professional jealousy was largely responsible. "You get your name in the newspapers all the time," one of Izzy's superiors complained, "whereas mine hardly ever gets mentioned. I must ask you to remember that you are merely a subordinate—not the whole show."

Bacchus opens the gates of the heart.
—HORACE

On November 13, 1925, the two agents were dismissed "for the good of the service." A bureau spokesman solemnly declared: "The service must be dignified. Izzy and Moe belong on the vaudeville stage."

Few New Yorkers ever pursued a humbler trade than the Gowanus Canal "woodchuck." It consisted of scrounging logs washed ashore from the fetid little waterway skirting South Brooklyn and peddling them for firewood. In 1919, Edward Donegan was a Gowanus Canal woodchuck with a wife and three children to support. In 1920, he was a Croesus, maintaining two establishments—one for his family and another for his mistress—and banking as much as $500,000 a month.

Donegan achieved his rapid change of fortune with the aid of a bevy of women employed in the office of the New York State prohibition director, Charles R. O'Connor. As a precaution against fraudulent withdrawal permits, the Prohibition Bureau had instituted a new rule requiring every bonded liquor warehouse and distillery, upon receipt of a permittee's order, to wire the state director for confirmation of its authenticity. The telegrams addressed to O'Connor passed through the hands of a 21-year-old clerk named Regina Sassone, and it was her responsibility to check the permits and reply to the telegrams. How Donegan in his lowly station learned of this system and saw a way to exploit it, how he raised the initial capital and made his first contacts inside O'Connor's office are not known, but early in 1920 he managed to meet and charm Regina Sassone. Ha lavished gifts and money upon her, set her up in a room at the Hotel McAlpin and, in the words of a federal court judge, "debauched her." When, thereafter, Regina received a distiller's query, she would notify her lover and delay the reply.

Thus armed, Donegan would adopt one of two courses. If the permit proved genuine, he would approach the permittee, posing as a prohibition official, deplore the bureaucratic red tape that was holding up the answering wire to the distillery, and promise to expedite matters for a fee. Most of the time he got it. In the case of spurious permits, he would first berate the offender for attempting to swindle the government and threaten to arrest him, then propose a payment of perhaps $20 a case as the only way to insure authentication of the permit. If he agreed, Regina would type the confirming telegram, affix Director O'Connor's rubber-stamp signature and let Donegan take it to a Western Union office for transmission to the distiller. He paid her $100 a telegram, no munificent recompense considering that such messages released thousands of cases of liquor worth millions of dollars.

The second clerk whom Donegan subverted was a Mrs. Mary Parkins, aged 38. She, in turn, recruited other clerks, as well as a dry agent or two. Donegan established her in a room adjoining Regina's, and with the door open between the two rooms, they became his headquarters.

Donegan presently altered his *modus operandi*. He began dealing directly with bootleggers, selling them forged or stolen permits obtained through his bureau friends, and, when they placed their

"In case you're interested, we passed Leavenworth two days ago."

order, seeing to it that Regina returned a favorable answer to the inquiry from the distillery.

What eventually aroused the suspicions of Chief Elmer Irey's Intelligence Unit were the sumptuous parties Mary Parkins gave at the McAlpin. Among the guests there appeared one day Agent Harold Stephenson from Washington. Secure in his conviction that every man had a price, Donegan offered him $10,000 if he could produce a permit to withdraw 100 barrels of whiskey. Stephenson promised to consider the proposition. Instead, he reported the offer to Irey. A few days later an Intelligence Unit agent, Walter P. Murphy, accompanied by three other agents, arrested Donegan in the Hotel McAlpin suite. Searching him, they found a revolver, a deputy sheriff's badge, $45,000 in cash, and a sheaf of distillers' telegrams querying O'Connor about permits which, if honored, would have unfrozen more than $4 million worth of whiskey.

Donegan was not perturbed. As the agents later deposed, when Murphy handed back the $45,000, Donegan asked him, "How about five grand to fix this thing up?"

Murphy feigned innocence. "We're from Washington. We're not onto your New York slang. We don't know what you mean."

Donegan showed them. He peeled off five $1,000 bills and added $1,500 more for good measure. He then turned his back, coyly assuring the agents, "I'm not seeing anything." They marked the bills as evidence and charged Donegan with attempted bribery.

Donegan raised his offer to $25,000 and began stuffing bills into Murphy's overcoat. When this failed to move the agents, he called to a man waiting in the other room, a recently acquired member of his ring. Samuel Bien, alias Sigmund "Beansie" Rosenfeld—"the Honorable Rosenfeld," he liked to be called—a card shark and gambling house operator, had been serving a prison term a few months earlier when he was pardoned because of failing health. He promptly joined the Donegan ring. Beansie's pockets, too, bulged with distillers' telegrams as he entered the suite. Assessing the situation at a glance, he held up a reassuring hand. "You don't know how to handle a thing like this, Eddie," he told Donegan (according to Murphy's report). "Let me handle this." He stepped up confidently to the agents. "I am placed in a very embarrassing position. I've dealt with all sorts of officials—city, state and federal—and I want to fix this thing up. I'll give you fellows twenty-five grand and two bucks on every case we move. This is too sweet a racket to break up. And you won't be in any danger. I'll pay it through a third party. Anybody you say. A lawyer, a politician, anybody." The agents made no sound or motion other than to jot down Beansie's remarks.

"Look, fellows," he went on, "don't be silly. If I don't keep my word, do you know what you can do? You can arrest me."

They didn't wait. They delivered Beansie to justice along with Donegan, Regina Sassone and Mary Parkins. Their combined bail was set at $250,000, which Donegan produced within a few minutes. A federal grand jury indicted the foursome for stealing government documents and conspiring to violate the Volstead Act. In addition, the Internal Revenue Service filed a claim of $1,635,797 against Donegan for taxes due on his 1920 income, plus penalties. It was a historic tax claim—the first brought against a bootlegger.

Beansie Rosenfeld died in February, 1922, three weeks before the trial. The charges against Mary Parkins were dropped when she turned state's witness. William Fallon, the flashiest trial lawyer of his day—"the Great Mouthpiece"—defended Donegan. Regina made a full confession on the witness stand, and the jury, sympathetically viewing her as a victim of seduction, acquitted her. Donegan they speedily convicted. The judge fined him $65,000 and sentenced him to ten years in the Atlanta penitentiary. "I paid them lawyers two hundred thousand bucks and got ten years," Donegan said after the appellate court confirmed the verdict. "A hundred-buck Brooklyn lawyer would have gotten me half that and been glad to wait for his money."

At the extreme opposite end of the New York social scale from the ex-Gowanus woodchuck were the four dashing La Montagne brothers. Scions of old-line French vintners with affiliates on both sides of the Atlantic, they had achieved distinction as businessmen, sportsmen and *Social Register*ites. They held memberships in a dozen elite Manhattan and Long Island clubs, including the Racquet and Tennis, the Piping Rock, the Knickerbocker and the Brook. Through the marriage of a cousin they were related to the illustrious president of Columbia University, Nicholas Murray Butler. Montaigu, the eldest La Montagne brother, an accomplished horseman, maintained his legal residence in France—the Château de Grandbourg at Evry Petit Bourg near Paris. Morgan, named after an uncle who owned a fleet of cargo vessels, occupied a suite at the Hotel Weylin near Park Avenue, while René, a seven-goal polo player who headed the United States team during the 1914 series against England, shared his apartment with the youngest La Montagne, William, a Yale graduate.

From their father, René Sr., the brothers had inherited the international liquor concern of E. La Montagne's Sons, Inc., which controlled both the Green River Distilling Company and the Eminence Distilling Company. When prohibition came, they saw no reason to abandon the traditional family pursuit. Had not their celebrated in-law, Dr. Butler, declared that the Volstead Act contravened the will of the people and so to violate it could constitute no offense against society?

The La Montagnes became the only bootleggers of impeccable social status in the annals of prohibition. Permits obtained through their connections in government circles enabled them to withdraw

---

 Wanna Make Manitoba Moonshine?   Have you ever wanted to make Canadian whiskey out of cheap stock? Well, just take a fifth of the lowest-priced American whiskey, add 1½ ounces of port wine, shake well, and let stand for about three hours.
It's a nice little process if you're broke or in need of a hobby.

---

the liquor from the distilleries they controlled and to supply scores of New York's fashionable hotels, cabarets and private clubs. Already prosperous before 1920, they amassed a fortune during the first three years of the decade at the rate of $2 million a year.

What finally brought the brothers to grief was a bachelor dinner given late in 1922 at the Racquet and Tennis Club by a fellow member named Bartow. The brothers provided the champagne. A disgruntled employee of E. La Montagne's Sons, Inc., reported the affair to an assistant U.S. attorney, Major John Holley Clark Jr., claiming, though unable to name them, that several federal officials were accomplices. Summoning the brothers, Clark offered them immunity if they would identify the officials. They haughtily declined and were indicted.

At first the brothers pleaded not guilty, but when they realized that many Racquet and Tennis Club confreres would have to testify, to spare them embarrassment they did the gentlemanly thing and changed their plea. "According to several commentators," reported *The New York Times*, "high society has been shocked." But if shocked, it was not so much by the brothers' bootlegging as by the consequent stoppage of excellent liquor. Luminaries of high society in New York and Washington flocked to their aid. "Every conceivable political and personal appeal, including an appeal by a Cabinet officer, was made to quash the case," Assistant Attorney General Willebrandt revealed.

The federal court meted out relatively light sentences—a $2,000 fine for each brother, four months in the Essex County jail for René, Morgan and William and two months for Montaigu.

The *Social Register* continued to list the La Montagne brothers until 1929, then dropped them forever. President Coolidge, on the other hand, personally restored the citizenship rights they had forfeited as convicts.

A large new class of offenders had been created by prohibition. It was a class distinct from the professional mobsters, the Al Capones, the Jack Diamonds, the Dutch Schultzes, for whom prohibition offered only an additional, though by far the most productive, source of easy money. Before prohibition the mobsters' chief ventures consisted of robbery, extortion, and whoremongering, and after it they would also go heavily into labor-industrial rackets and gambling. But many bootleggers had no general felonious proclivity. Without the Volstead Act, their names might never have appeared on a police blotter. They eschewed terrorism as a business practice, sold drinkable liquor and saw no basic moral difference between themselves and their clients. The instant millionaires of bootlegging could cite commanding figures like Nicholas Murray Butler and Clarence Darrow. "The Eighteenth Amendment is an unenforceable law and a bad law," the latter contended. "It should be treated with contempt."

Even the most sanguine wets were astounded by the speed with which the states acted on the Twenty-first Amendment. On December 5, 1933, at 5:32 p.m., Washington time, Utah Convention delegate S. R. Thurman, having satisfied himself that the 35th state (Pennsylvania) had ratified, cast the last ballot for Utah. At seven o'clock, thirteen years, ten months and eighteen days after the Noble Experiment began, President Roosevelt signed the proclamation ending it.

Repeal came as something of an anticlimax. Because it came so late in the day, liquor trucks could not make many deliveries to hotels and nightclubs before closing time. The English liner *Majestic*, delayed at sea by a storm, with 6,200 cases in her hold, did not dock until morning. Most speakeasies, having survived a decade of illegality, declined to risk a penalty now by operating without a license, but the licensing officials could not handle all the paper work. The chairman of the New York State Alcohol Control Board, Edward P. Mulrooney, stayed at his desk all night, managing to validate barely 1,000 licenses. In Manhattan's Merry-Go-Round, the clientele groaned as the owner, Omar Champion, pressed a button, stopping the bar's rotation, had chicken netting thrown over it and a sign posted, NO DRINKS SERVED. "Not a drop till we're legal," he said, and the frustrated celebrants wandered off in search of a licensed water hole.

The marquee of Minsky's Burlesque on 42nd Street spelled out in lights WE'LL TAKE GIN, but the crowd in Times Square was far less boisterous than on any New Year's Eve. New Jersey's Governor A. Harry Moore vetoed a state liquor-control measure as unconstitutional, thereby postponing a legal drink for Jerseyites, but at the same time he remarked: "Liquor has been sold illegally for thirteen years in New Jersey, and it will not hurt if this is done for a few days more." New Orleans greeted repeal with cannon salvos lasting twenty minutes. In Baltimore, H. L. Mencken had his say, as usual: "It isn't often that anything to the public good issues out of American politicians. This time they have been forced to be decent." He then perversely tossed down a glass of water. "My first in thirteen years," he said.

drink to-day

by john fletcher

(1579–1625)

DRINK to-day and drown all sorrow,
You shall perhaps not do it to-morrow:
Best, while you have it, use your breath;
There'll be no drinking after death.

Wine works the heart up, wakes the wit,
There is no cure 'gainst age but it:
It helps the headache, cough and tisic,
And is for all diseases physic.

Then let us smile, boys, for our health;
Who drinks well, loves the commonwealth;
And he that will to bed go sober,
Falls with the leaf still in October.

If your mark on that first little drinking quiz revealed that you belong with Fresca, here's another chance to return to the bar with your head held high. This is a longer, harder quiz, so go ahead and guess a lot. The answers—which you might want to check before you start—are on the bottom of page 187.

another shot
at your alcoholic iq

HERE'S an alcohol test you can rate high on without being sent to the pokey. The names of thirteen intoxicating beverages are listed below. The idea is to match them up with the proper descriptions. A teetotaler probably won't be able to handle more than four or five; nine or ten rates you a very social drinker, and if you get all thirteen you're a real boozer.

1. LAGER	____a.	An alcoholic liquor distilled from wine.
2. BEER	____b.	Holland gin.
3. SAMSHU	____c.	A liquor made in Russia from rye, or sometimes from barley or potatoes.
4. ARRACK	____d.	A liquor distilled from fermented molasses or cane-juice.
5. GIN	____e.	A very dark brown heavy English malt liquor resembling beer.
6. SAKE	____f.	A brandy made from apples.
7. VODKA	____g.	A beer containing few hops.
8. RUM	____h.	An alcoholic liquor distilled in China from rice or millet.

9. BOURBON	____i.	An aromatic liquor concocted from various grains and flavored with juniper-berries.
10. APPLEJACK	____j.	An alcoholic liquor fermented from malt and hops.
11. BRANDY	____k.	A whiskey distilled from Indian corn and rye.
12. SCHNAPPS	____l.	A Japanese liquor distilled from rice.
13. PORTER	____m.	A strong Oriental drink concocted from the juice of the coco-palm, etc.

ANSWERS

1-g, 2-j, 3-h, 4-m, 5-i, 6-l, 7-c,
8-d, 9-k, 10-f, 11-a, 12-b, 13-e.

ANOTHER SHOT AT YOUR ALCOHOLIC IQ   187

"You tell your Mr. Ryan that I'm flattered,
but I already have a date for this evening."

Certain sober theologians may take issue with Benjamin Franklin's story of the origin of wine, but it seems divinely inspired to me.

10,000 b.c. war a very good year

"IN VINO VERITAS," Franklin wrote. "Before Noah, men, having only water to drink, could not find the truth. Accordingly, they became abominably wicked, and they were justly exterminated by the water they loved to drink. This good man, Noah, having seen that all his contemporaries had perished by this unpleasant drink, took a dislike to it; and God, to relieve his dryness, created the vine and revealed to him the art of making *le vin.* By the aid of this liquid he unveiled more and more truth; and since this time all the best things, even the gods, have been called *divine.*

"He made the wine to cheer us. When you see your neighbor at table pour wine into his glass do not hasten to pour water into it. Why would you drown truth? Know that the apostle Paul advised Timothy very seriously to put wine into his water for his health; but that not one of the apostles, nor any of the holy fathers, ever watered wine.

"P.S. In order to still more confirm you in your piety and recognition of divine providence, reflect on the position God has given the elbow. By its present location, we see it designed so that we can drink at our ease, with the glass coming just to the mouth. Let us then adore, glass in hand, that wise benevolence; let us adore and drink."

Here, in painting and prose, is a rich and merry history of that hallowed house of hullabaloo, the Western saloon. Old World bards have lavished eloquence on wine, but only an American drinking Bear's Milk could have asked

Who shot Maggie in the freckle?
Who shot Maggie in the divide?

This piece has more of the authentic flavor of the Old West than 50 John Wayne films; for, as Richard Erdoes says, "The history of the American West is told in its saloons."

how the west was wan — the morning after

by richard erdoes

A MOUNTAIN pass in Southern Colorado. The only man-made thing in sight is a disintegrating log cabin tilted drunkenly to one side with window holes like a skull's empty sockets. Inside, barely discernible in semidarkness, the shattered remains of rough, homemade chairs and tables, a floor covered with broken bottles iridescent with age, a battered spittoon, a cluster of bats hanging head down from the rafters. On the wall a faded sign:

Thirst
Comes first.
Drink till you burst!
Everything else can wait!

In the beginning there was the saloon. A tale is told of a whiskey peddler crossing the prairie with his oxcart. One day the oxen lay down and died. The peddler put his barrels of redeye in a semicircle out in the grass and painted "SALOON" on the nearest rock. Within three days a town grew up around it.

The Western Saloon and Western History—what would the one be without the other? Most of the West's spectaculars, the famous murders, duels, deeds of passion and acts of derring-do took place in whiskey-shops. Can one imagine Calamity Jane or Wild Bill Hickock anywhere else BUT in a saloon? It is true that the battle of the Little Bighorn took place outdoors, but it is the booze palaces which keep the memory of this event green in the minds of innumerable drinking men—and women—gazing at fly-specked Anheuser-Busch lithographs of "Custer's Last Stand" while downing their particular "brand of pizen."

A good Western saloon filled a great many needs besides being just a drinking establishment, gambling den and place for trafficking with hurdy-gurdy girls. It also often served as courthouse, hotel, way-station for stagecoaches, assayer's office, theater, political campaign headquarters, eatery and improvised jail. It was always in a saloon that a fledgling town's first religious services were held— the bar serving as the pulpit, beer kegs being used for church seats.

One well-known early evangelist, Jake the Saint, made a specialty of invading Arizona and New Mexico whiskey-mills with a Bible in one hand, a loaded six-gun in the other, exhorting sinful boozers to "Get down on your knees and yell!"

As far as dispensing justice in a barroom is concerned, the best known of many examples is probably Roy Bean's combination courthouse and saloon, The Jersey Lily, at Langtry, Texas, where old Bean tended bar as well as acting the judge. The mahogany counter, worn smooth by numberless elbows, was also the judge's bench. Bean invariably starting proceedings with a "Hear ye! Hear ye! This honorable court is now in session; and if any son of a bitch wants a snort afore we start, let him step up to the bar and name his brand!"

Bean's particular brand of justice was swift and merciless. Once, a stranger asked for a bottle of beer and plunked down a twenty-dollar gold piece. The judge gave him nineteen dollars in change. "What, a whole dollar for one bottle of beer?" objected the outraged customer. "You crazy, cheating old bastard!"

Judge Roy (I'm the Law west of the Pecos) Bean pulled a six-gun on the startled customer and roared: "Court will come to order! You're fined $6.66 2/3 for disturbing the peace; $6.66 2/3 for cussin' in public; and $6.66 2/3 for contempt of court. That's twenty bucks!" He then relaxed and in an unexplained fit of generosity announced: "The beer's on the house."

A Taos barkeeper, doubling as justice of the peace, loved to perform marriages. His rites were truly poetic:

> Under this roof in stormy weather,
> This Buck and Squaw now come together.
> Let none but HIM who rules the thunder,
> Pull this buck and squaw asunder!
>
> You are now properly wed, by Jove,
> And let's all have a drink.

In spite of all these extraneous activities, drinking was a saloon's main business. The universal drink was "Cowboy's Cocktail" —straight whiskey. Sissified, "educated" drinks were frowned upon. An unfortunate English dude rash enough to ask for Prickly Ash

Bitters to moisten his muttonchops in Tombstone's Crystal Palace was advised, at gunpoint, "To make it straight whiskey, or we'll make a hole in your skull and pour it in!"

But, then, there is whiskey and whiskey. Old Joe Gideon was prefered by the fastidious and well-heeled. Other varieties were less smooth. There was Taos Lightning—guaranteed to strike you dead on the spot. Skull-Bender was a brand dispensed at Custer City at two bits a glass. It had a reputation of inducing the most stupendous hangovers known to man. There was Valley Tan, also known as Mormon Juice—because it made a man see his wife triple, inspiring polygamic hallucinations. Old Forty Rod was so named because it brought its man down at exactly that distance. Bumblebee Whiskey—the drink with sting, Brave-Maker, Conversation Fluid, Gut-Warmer, Red-Eye, Tarantula Juice, Grizzly Bear's Milk, Tonsil Tickler, Tornado Juice, Nose-Paint . . . the varieties were endless. According to an ancient miner who had sampled every brand, all early Western firewater was vile, virile and vigorous. One of the most haunting descriptions of its flavor and effect is Irwin S. Cobb's description of a special brand of corn-likker drunk at Abilene and Dodge City: "It smells like gangrene starting in a mildewed silo, it tastes like the wrath to come, and when you absorb a deep swig of it you have all the sensations of having swallowed a lighted kerosene lamp. A sudden, violent jolt of it has been known to stop the victim's watch, snap his suspenders and crack his glass eye right across."

Oldtimers pronounced Snakehead Whiskey—also known as Rattlesnake Piss—the most deadly of all brews. One or two heads of prairie rattlers put into each barrel endowed this kind of whiskey with its special potency. It was given an extra kick by the addition of a large plug of chawing tobaccer and a tablespoon of gunpowder. Thus fortified it was known as Red Uprising and said to draw a blood blister on a rawhide boot. It inspired one of the favorite cowboy toasts:

> *Up to my lips and over my gums:*
> *Look out guts, here she comes!*

It made frying-size men challenge a multitude of giants: "I got two rows of nipples an' holes bored for more. I pull up trees by the roots an' if a mountain gits in my way, I jest kick her to one side. I'm a rarin', tarin' cyclone of chain-lightning loaded with destruction. I'm the idol of all wimmin and bad news to their men!"

Beer was drunk as a chaser—"Give me a boilermaker with his helper"—but miners could get drunk on beer alone. In the long-extinct Philadelphia Beer Parlor in Bodie, California ("the wickedest

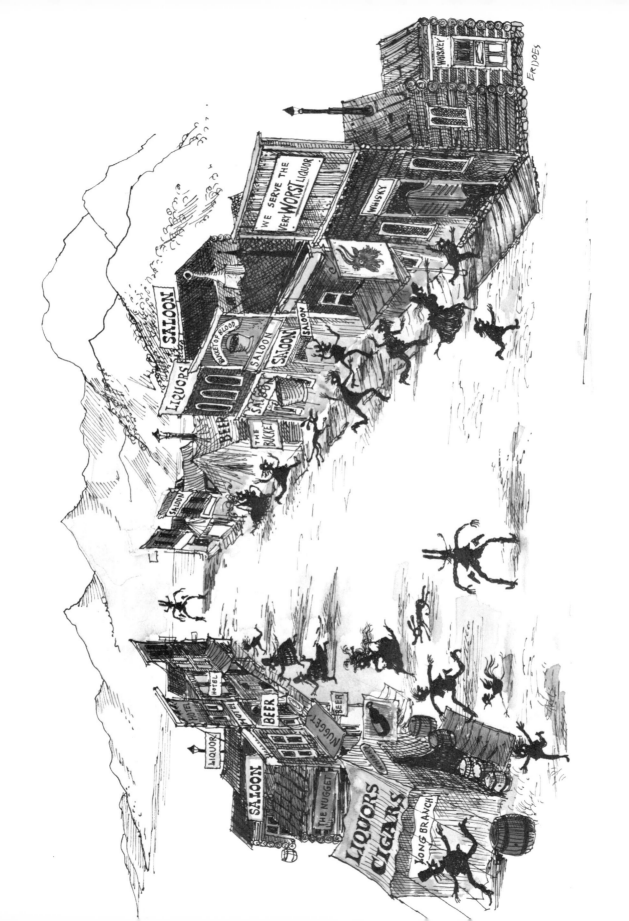

groggery in the Far West's most wicked city") teams from various mining camps held epic contests trying to drink each other under the table. Here, miners brought in the skeleton of a dear, departed comrade and ask that it be given a drink: "Fill him up to the top, like he always liked it." Beer was served in huge mugs for a nickel to anybody of age or tall enough to put his chin on the counter.

The legendary, historic saloons, what has become of them? Shorty Young's original Bucket of Blood in Le Havre, Montana, and its several namesakes: the Long Branch of Dodge City—the Beautiful, Bibulous Babylon of the Plains; Leadville's Pioneer Club; Nuthall & Mann's famous Number Ten in Deadwood; the Exchange

And to tell you the truth
It is not the vermouth.
I think that perhaps it's the gin.

—OGDEN NASH

in Creede; Tombstone's Crystal Palace; Aspen's Red Onion; Georgetown's Red Ram; or Fort Whoop-Up at Shelby, Montana, which straddled the U.S.–Canadian border in order to discombobulate the law: If a Mountie entered the establishment, evil-doers retreated to the saloon's American half. If a U.S. marshal came through the swinging doors customers retreated to the Canadian side. The Nugget, the Silver Dollar, Maggie's Place, the Antlers in San Antonio with its famous sign: "Get Pickled Here," what was their fate?

To find out, I conducted my very own Archaeological Expedition of Alcoholic Antiquities. Alas, some of the far-famed booze parlors have crumbled into dust—ruins inhabited by bats and owls, though sometimes not without a faint trace of former grandeur. Some have vanished altogether. Others underwent a sort of reincarnation. The building is gone, but the bar and its original fittings and decor have been saved to be resurrected in another place. The ornate bar from a Denver house of ill-fame has found a new lease on life in a small-town Elks Club. A hundred years ago four beauteous, sparkling girl bartenders worked behind its shiny hardwood counter serving drinks and "also tending to other diverse wants of numerous gentlemen guests." There is only one bartender now and he is fat, gloomy and male.

Happily, dozens of the grand old places are still in business at their original location, their appearance unchanged, diffusing a joyful glow of contentment among the drinking public. A good place to start is Georgetown, Colorado, the "Silver Queen of the Rockies," a town of many quaint, Victorian buildings. In 1864 it boasted of four cabins, a few prospectors' tents and three dugouts, and proudly proclaimed itself a town. One gold-seeker, George Griffith, named the baby metropolis after himself. Then came the boom as silver fever brought in multitudes of newcomers.

> The miners came in '49,
> The whores in '61,
> They rolled upon the barroom floor,
> and made the native son

as one song has it. By 1868 the town had a newspaper, which complained: "Last year Georgetown gave steady support to no less than 13 whiskey shops, and yet it was found impossible to keep one school running!"—the history of the Old West in a nutshell. What the reporter forgot to mention were the five high-class cat houses, 11 cribs, and dozen gambling dens. Mollie Dean and Mattie Estes were the two foremost madams, having imported "Numerous Brides of the Multitude." In Georgetown's private collections are two brass tokens which were used to pay for the services of shady ladies. Both show the portrait of a beautiful girl with luxurious ringlets falling to her bare shoulders. The reverse side of one of the tokens reads: "Mattie's Place—good for one Screw." The inscription on the other token says:

> $ 1. Lookee
> $ 2. Feelee
> $ 3. Dooee.
> Compliments of Mme Ruth Jacobs

But I am digressing, carried away by Georgetown's purple past. The city's oldest drinking establishment is the Red Ram, which still advertises itself as the oldest bar in Colorado. Its bullet-scarred bar was hauled by oxcart across the Kansas Plains in 1859. So were the large, diamond-dust French mirrors. The Red Ram's first owner was illiterate. He also got into an argument with his sign painter. As a result the legend across the saloon's front read: "We sell the *VERY WORST* whiskey!" For unexplained reasons this sign attracted huge crowds of miners and the place became a great success. In 1867 the first church services were held here: "No booze for thirty minutes, boys, the padre's got a few words to say." During the sermon the picture of the nude lady over the counter was chastely covered with burlap.

As to those artfully done oil paintings of disrobed sirens which grace most of the Western saloons it should be remarked that the beauties depicted are generally shaped like bass fiddles—the ideal female of the time. As one proud man described his ladylove: "I can span her waist in my two hands, but she couldn't sit down in a tub."

Other notable events taking place in Georgetown's saloons were faithfully reported in the *Colorado Miner*: "Yesterday James Feehan

---

Do You Have to Order by Western Union?   The longest bar in the world is 287 feet and is at the Working Men's Club of Mildura in Victoria, Australia. It has thirty-two pumps.

---

shot Thomas Mulqueen in the leg, whereupon Mulqueen bit Feehan's lower lip off. Also, President Grant and party will arrive friday evening." Social affairs in Georgetown's drinking places were indeed dazzling: "Yesterday an assembly took place which for beauty and refinement has never been equaled in our lovely valley. The gentlemen were dressed in the latest fashion. Dan Mullharon wore a full dress suit of broadcloth and had his shoes blackened. The beautiful, dusky Mrs. Chipeta wore a dress of Lyonnaise velvet and a sealskin sack. Even then she complained of the cold, but we imagine it was because she was not accustomed to the altitude. Mr. Colorow, who accompanied Mrs. Chipeta, wore a Prince Albert coat made of an old army blanket and buckskin breeches. His hair was dressed à la Oscar Wilde or an Indian herb doctor."

The Red Ram has plenty of atmosphere and an excellent cuisine. Frequently the McClellan Players will stroll into the place after having finished their old-fashioned "Meller-drama." I saw them downing huge beakers of beer still dressed in their costumes. Tacked on the wall I discovered an old, yellowed advertisement: "Selak's celebrated ale. Takes right hold of the vitals and elevates the soul. It opens the faculties, tickles the fountains of charity, clears the canals of the heart and strikes down to the very bottom of contentedness." The drinks in the Red Ram affected me in a similar way. My contentment was heightened by some of the actors and guests joining in an impromptu chorus:

And when my work is over, to Cheyenne then I'll head,
Fill up on beer and whiskey and paint the damn town red!
Drink that rotgut, drink that rednose when you get to town,
Drink it straight, and swig it mighty, till the world goes round and
*   round.*

During the first two or three years of a mining town's existence, saloons and living quarters were primitive—to put it mildly. A crude sign in Virginia City during the height of the Comstock craze read:

No beds to be had.
Horse blanket in an old sugar hogshead, per night, $10.
Crockery crate, with straw, $7.50
Without straw, $5.75
For cellar door, $4.
Vacant sheep corral, 4 bits.

But all this changed with wonderful swiftness due to the immense wealth in gold and silver gushing from the mines and within a few years ornate, well-appointed bars, eateries, hotels, even opera houses began to grow from amid tents and dugouts. Georgetown's Hotel de Paris, now a museum, is a fine example and still a classic Western landmark. It was built by Louis Dupuy, known as "French Louis." Born in Alençon of wealthy parents, he was a deserter from Napoleon the Third's army and later from the U.S. cavalry, a sometimes journalist, philosopher, atheist, anarchist, miner, gourmet, master-cook, conversationalist, but especially a man who hated taxes and women. For over 25 years he devoted his life to the civilization of rough Westerners, especially to their culinary education. He is known as the "Father of Domestic Science in America." As a hotel-keeper Dupuy insisted on grace and style. Guests who did not measure up to his old-world standards found themselves forcefully ejected. He used to say that he would rather let a room to a fastidious, well-mannered whore, than to the dowdy, ill-bred wife of a millionaire mine owner. . . . .

The wines in Monsieur Dupuy's cellar were choice. He even had a full assortment of champagne, called "Giggle Soup" by the local jokels. Mr. Dupuy died defiantly without ever having paid a penny in taxes, a true Frenchman to the last, and now rests side by side with his lady companion under a stone which simply reads: DEUX BONS AMIS. He was lucky that the town had finally, in 1886, gotten around to establishing a cemetery. At the grand opening a corpse was lacking, and so a horsethief was hurriedly hanged to inaugurate the Bone Orchard in style.

Not every town had its Dupuy. A resident of Deadwood, South Dakota, complained:

The beefsteak is of leather,
The pies are made of tin,
The bacon you couldn't cut with a sword,
The coffee's very thin,
In the little one-horse hash-house where I board.

Legendary Deadwood, deep in the Black Hills, stolen from the Sioux, where "Thar was gold in the very grass-roots and a man couldn't take a leak properly without stumbling and falling over some fist-sized nuggets strewn about the landscape." Deadwood, where every shifting breeze was laden with an aroma of malt and strong waters, where shaggy-bearded miners downed enormous hookers of straight rye followed by a tall beer as a chaser. Deadwood, city of desperados, gunslingers, bunco-steerers and wilted lilies of the prairie, where saloons outnumbered all other buildings five to one, a town which after its first year of existence contained no less than 75 whiskey-mills.

Some Deadwoodians spent almost their whole lives inside the saloons . . . "They went in and never came out again." This, supposedly, was on account of the lack of paved streets: "Deadwood mud has a special, rich quality, its adhesive properties are rare, its depth unfathomable, its color indefinable, its extent illimitable, its usefulness unknown."

One of Deadwood's most notorious drinking places was the Green Front, hangout of Martha Jane Canary, better known as Calamity Jane. She claimed to have received her nickname after rescuing a lover from the hands of ferocious Indians—"saving him from dire calamity." People who disliked her claimed that she got her name because "men were stricken by a venereal calamity shortly after making her acquaintance." She wore men's clothes, chewed tobacco, was usually high on Dakota Dynamite and had "a brilliant vocabulary never learned at her mother's knee." She shot up many a

---

Foam on the Range   The largest beer-selling establishment in the world is the Mathaser at Bayerstrasse 5 in Munich, where the daily sale reaches 84,470 pints.

---

bar and blackened the eyes of more than one officer of the law. She boasted of having been fired from a Bozeman, Montana, parlor house "for being a bad influence on the other girls."

Another lady haunting the saloons of Deadwood was La Belle Siddons, alias Madame Vestal, alias Lurline Monte Verde—the Gambling Queen. "Then there is Monte Verde, with her dark eyes and tresses, who on her arrival in Deadwood stood on a board and was born through the town on the shoulders of four strapping miners, and who now deals "21" and dances the jig with a far-off look in her left eye." That eye, as it turned out, was on Archie

McLaughlin, Ex-Quantrell raider and road agent. If a lucky gambler left Monte Verde's place with a big haul of money, she tipped off her ever-loving Archie who promptly relieved him of his winnings at gunpoint. At Monte Verde's the odds favored the house. But Archie died from a throat ailment, being hanged by an irate mob of vigilante gamblers. Monte Verde swallowed poison, and when that didn't kill her she simply tried to drink herself to death. She finally faded from Deadwood, though not from memory.

Another frequenter of Deadwood's bars was Madame Featherlegs who used to gallop through town on a wall-eyed bronc in her bright red underwear, her skirts hitched up to her navel. The long-johns were much frazzled from daily hard-riding, hence the lady's nickname.

Nor should a beautiful nymph called "Tidbit" be forgotten, she who had the names of her many lovers embroidered on her dress. Those who graced her bosom were nearest to her heart, while those whose names appeared on the place on which she sat knew themselves to be out of favor.

Two theatres, La Bella Donna and the Gem, dispensed culture as well as whiskey. On a wintry night, during a howling snowstorm, an ice-encrusted figure staggered into La Bella Donna interrupting a golden-haired songstress during her rendition of "The Rose upon my Sainted Mother's Grave," by emptying his six-shooter at the piano player. All shots missed, for the intruder's fingers were stiff and numb. The pianist, whirling on his stool, fired one single shot—and did not miss. The beautiful singer broke into sobs, screaming: "Oh, John, he has killed you!" The dying John turned out to be the husband of the golden-haired warbler, who had left him for the nimble-fingered musician. Expiring, the poor man exhorted the sinful couple to "at least get properly married after he went up the flume." They promised and John contentedly cashed in his chips. The onlooking miners shed buckets of tears while the wedding promptly took place. The sadly joyful event was celebrated by downing great quantities of good old Joe Gideon.

There was seldom a dull moment in a Black Hills groggery. In Manning's Saloon, one Frank McGovern got into a friendly argument with the bartender who shot him in the face with his revolver. The bullet hit McGovern squarely in the center of the forehead, traveled upwards between scalp and skull and came out at the top of his head. McGovern was slightly shaken, but none the worse for wear. I mention this incident only to foster some historical speculation of whether the victim could have been an ancestor of South Dakota's favorite son.

Deadwood's most famous saloon was Nuttal and Mann's Number Ten, the favorite hangout of Wild Bill Hickock, the Prince of the Pistoleers, the "mildest man that ever scuttled ship or cut a throat." Many people know that he killed 27 men. Fewer are aware that, together with Sitting Bull and other Western heroes, he also starred in Eastern cities in Buffalo Bill's Wild West Show. As a circus performer Wild Bill was a total failure. With the spotlight on him, he

Skoal and Blast Off!   The longest distance for a champagne cork to fly from an untreated and unheated bottle four feet from level ground is 73 feet, 10½ inches, popped by A. D. Beaty at Hever, Kent, England on July 20, 1971.

was felled by stage fright and unable to utter a sound. Maybe the words he was supposed to utter had something to do with it: "Fear not, fair maid, you are safe at last with Wild Bill, who is ready to risk his life, if need be, in the defense of weak and helpless womanhood." Wild Bill, at any rate, choked and went back to what he could do best—playing poker and killing people. He planned to accept the job of marshal in Deadwood. Not wanting their city cleaned up and aware of Hickock's reputation as a killer, (but not of the fact that he was going blind) the citizens hired Jack McCall, a tinhorn gambler, to murder him.

Wild Bill was shot through the brain while playing poker in old Number Ten, sitting with his back to the door, something he usually managed to avoid. He was holding what has since become known as the "Dead Man's Hand"—black aces, black eights, and the Jack of Diamonds. The bullet which passed through Hickock's head went on to lodge in the wrist of his poker partner Frank Massey. Frank later used to enter saloons with the triumphant exclamation: "Gentlemen, the bullet that killed Wild Bill has come to town!" As to the murderer, Jack McCall, he eventually died of "Hemp Fever."

> Oh, bury me with my knife and six-shooter,
> My spurs at my heels, my rifle at my side;
> And place on my coffin a bottle of brandy,
> For my ghost to swallow, when he goes for a ride.

Wild Bill was planted in Deadwood's boothill and his grave is one of the Black Hills' great tourist attractions. His original monument has been chipped away, piece by piece, by souvenir hunters. When Calamity Jane died many years later her last words were: "Bury me

next to Bill," and so they rest side by side. "It's a good thing Bill is dead," commented an old friend. "He'd never have stood for this! He never liked her!"

What's left besides memories? Old Number Ten, for one, now also known as Old-Style Saloon. Its exterior is largely rebuilt and Disneyed up, but the inside is still pure Golden West, even though the drinkers whose elbows wear out the beautiful old Brunswicke-Callander bar now wear sunglasses and hot pants. Hanging above the door is the chair in which Wild Bill met his doom and the place is literally chockfull with mementos. Number Ten is a gratifyingly typical old whiskey-mill. The walls are covered with stuffed specimens of everything that runs, crawls, swims, or flies in the Dakotas, trophies mostly shot by appreciative customers. There is also a profusion of miners' picks and shovels, ore specimens, crystals and fossils, besides an assortment of shooting irons. The busts of Deadwood's more notorious characters gaze down upon the drinking public from a shelf above the bar. The memory of Wild Bill is kept fresh by frequent melodramatic reenactments of the trial and hanging of Jack McCall.

Another survivor is the Buffalo Bar. It has huge, stuffed buffalo heads, buffalo skins, buffalo mosaics made of dimes and nickels, buffalos on the ceiling made of ropes and lassos, and buffalo statues and it serves, appropriately, buffalo steaks and buffaloburgers. It also proudly displays the famous "Face on the Barroom Floor," recalling the well-known song:

'Twas a balmy summer evening and a goodly crowd was there,
Which well-nigh filled Joe's barroom, on the corner of the square;
And as songs and racy stories came through the open door,
A vagabond crept slowly in and sank upon the floor . . .

According to legend, the vagabond had once been a wealthy, far-famed artist whose wife ran away with another man. Since then he had been searching for her, sinking lower and lower. With his last ounce of strength, and a few bits of colored chalk, he sketched his wife's likeness on the floor, cried out, "Does someone here know her?" and died. It is only fair to point out that there are a number of saloons claiming to own "the one, original genuine Face on the Barroom Floor. . . .

Vigorous drinking is still practiced throughout the Black Hills in Lead, Rockerville, Hill City, Silver City and Custer. Near Custer, miners once came across the body of a woman with an arrow through her back, her hand still clutching a five-dollar bill. The pious men decided that "it waren't fittin' for the lady to meet her maker with a fiver in her hand," and they thoughtfully removed the note before giving her an on-the-spot funeral. The money, it was decided, should go to charity—but which one?

The question was debated at length in Custer's old McHugh's Saloon, when one man's eye was caught by a sign advertising Skull-Bender Whiskey at two bits a glass. A great light began to dawn on him. There were twenty men in the burial party. Would not the dear, departed sister, looking down upon them from up high, think that the greatest act of charity toward a body of hot perspiring, dry-throated miners who had just done their bit of shoveling was to provide them with some means to moisten their dryness? God's finger was immediately perceived in the fact that twenty men with five bucks to spend had exactly enough for a skull-bender apiece. Such is the stuff miracles are made of. All great events in the life of Custer City somehow took place in, or in front of, or within walking distance of Bill McHugh's Saloon—such as an impromptu necktie party for a local badman called Fly Specked Billy—a spectacle nightly reenacted during the tourist season. Old McHugh's is gone, but other saloons have risen in its place and its spirit liveth. . . .

Sheridan, Wyoming, is another town after the Western saloon buff's heart. The Mint Bar fits the pattern of a typical old-style, nontourist stockman's saloon. "The hardwood counter runs lengthwise on the right and can be as much as 50 or 60 feet long. It has a brass footrail with spittoons placed at regular intervals for the convenience of the chewing public. Sawdust is sprinkled generously

---

He Must Have Put It on His Master Charge   The highest price ever paid for a bottle of wine of any size is $9,200 for a jeroboam of Château Mouton-Rothschild 1929 sold by Michael Noble, Britain's minister for trade, at Parke-Bernet Galleries in New York on May 23, 1972. This bottle contained the equivalent of five normal bottles and thus cost about $300 per glass or $25 a sip.

---

about the floor to absorb the drippings. On the sober side of the counter is the bardog, or professor, yawning on the glasses to give them a polish. The place is crowded with customers bellying up to the bar, a bunch of loose-tongued humans, airin' their lungs, looking down the neck of a bottle, getting callouses on their elbows from leaning on the counter. Now and then a cowhand shambles in, or out, with unsteady gait. Someone has stolen his rudder."

This description from the turn of the century fits the Mint Bar to a

T, except that, nowadays, it gets along without the sawdust. The walls are made of red cedar, so the bartender tells me. It is hard to tell, because they are absolutely covered with memorabilia: A stuffed moose head, stuffed coyotes, wolves, wolverines, foxes and owls, a huge, stuffed fish with wicked teeth, the skin of the largest rattle-

---

Go Liberate Somebody Else   In the three months before his libera-
tion, one prisoner in the Bastille consumed 12 bottles of brandy, 121 bottles of beer, and 167 bottles of wine.

---

snake ever, a pair of enormous longhorns, varmint traps, cowboy gear, chromos of unshucked lovelies, besides numberless faded, yellowed photographs of round-ups, brandings, stampedes, bronc-busting, Indian-fighting, old Cheyenne chiefs and other Wyoming scenes. The original ceiling is made of pressed, ornamental imitation leather. What little wood is visible has thousands of different cattle-brands burned into it. Booths are made out of some sort of gnarled, twisted wood and black-and-white calf skins.

The owner was happy to let me take some pictures, but as soon as the flash went off one irate customer jumped off his stool and threatened to take a swing at me. It seemed that his lady companion was not his wife and that he suspected me of being some sort of detective gathering material for a divorce case. I talked fast, explaining while dodging his blow, that I had traveled 2,000 miles just to take a picture of the famous Mint Bar. "Dog-gone, why din't ya say so! This is the best bar in Sheridan, in all Wyoming, in the whole West. Goldurn, blame my kittens, if you ain't the man. Put 'er there, y' blamed critter. Nominate your pizen!" They actually still talk that way in the Mint Bar.

By contrast the Buffalo Bill Bar is elegant and grammatically advanced, catering to the well-heeled dude. The Buffalo Bill Bar is the heart and soul of the historic Sheridan Inn, also known as the House of 69 Gables. The inn was opened in 1893 and had the first electric lights in all of Sheridan and for hundreds of miles around. Electricity was made by a coal-burning thrashing machine in the backyard. The whole town turned out to see the lights go on and to stare at the inn's two bathtubs, the first in that part of the state. . . .

While the Buffalo Bill Saloon and the Mint Bar are flourishing in the bloom of eternal youth, the notorious hog ranches are gone forever—and a good thing, too. A hog ranch, at first, was simply a place where hogs were raised and butchered, something frowned upon by cattlemen who looked upon pigs and sheep as malodorous abominations. Hog ranches often were divided into stalls which could be made into primitive "cribs" where so-called soiled doves catered to the physical needs of lonesome cowhands. With such a place always went a still distilling a particularly vile variety of tarantula juice. A hog ranch was booze and sex in the raw without rustling silk and velvet ribbons. The queen of hog ranches was Ella Watson, better known as Cattle Kate or Winchester Kate because of her proficiency with a rifle. Kate was a huge-breasted woman who straddled her horse in a flowery cotton dress and flapping sunbonnet. She made a habit of being paid in kind—accepting "motherless calves" instead of cash for her favors—and soon had a sizable herd of cattle. This annoyed the cattle-owners. One day six men with guns raided Cattle Kate and hanged her from a tree together with her sweetheart Jim Averell, sometime surveyor, pimp, saloonkeeper, justice of the peace and suspected rustler. The men who committed this brutal murder prided themselves of being solid citizens and taxpayers. The hog ranches disappeared, not because they offended morality, but because those who ran them were looked upon as fences for stolen cattle.

While a hog ranch was the lowest form of combination bar and brothel, the profession of saloon-keeper rose in the public estimation when Count and Countess Murat opened a bar and gambling house in Denver. The count claimed to be a descendent of Joachim Murat, Marshal of France, King of Naples and brother-in-law of the emperor Napoleon. The countess took in washing on the side and the count, besides pouring drinks, also did a little barbering. He once charged Horace Greeley five dollars for a shave.

A surprising number of venerable, historic saloons have been able to survive as part of equally venerable hotels. These places have a particular charm of their own. In them one can combine saloon-studying with good eating and lodging surrounded by plenty of atmosphere. One cannot find an old sign like this in a modern motel:

> THIS HOUSE IS STRICTLY INTEMPERATE.
> NONE BUT THE BRAVE DESERVE THE FARE.
> NO SHOOTING, UNLESS IN SELF-DEFENSE.
> PERSONS OWING BILLS FOR BOARD WILL BE BORED FOR BILLS.
> NO MORE THAN FIVE TO A BED.
> SHEETS WILL BE CHANGED NIGHTLY—ONCE A MONTH.
> WHEN BEDDING DOWN REMOVE YOUR SPURS, IT'S HARD
>   ON THE SHEETS.
> ALL MONIES TO BE LEFT WITH THE CLERK AS HE IS
>   NOT RESPONSIBLE.

or this one:

A word to the wise: All confidence sharks,
Thimble-riggers, Bunco-steerers, Sure-thing men
and all other objectionable characters:
STAY AWAY! (or face drastic action)

The nature of the action is not specified. Or, finally:

Snacks—two bits.
Square meal—four bits.
Belly Ache—one dollar.

The Grand Imperial in Silverton, Colorado, is a place with class. Though it still looks exactly as it did on opening day in 1883, it now has all the comforts of a modern hotel. It houses one of the West's finest old bars, the Hub Saloon, which traditionally never closes its doors. Its huge, beautiful cherrywood bar was shipped, bit by bit, on muleback, from Denver over the high mountain passes. It is flanked by large horseshoe mirrors imported from France. The ancient tables are marble-topped and the quality of the booze matches that of the furnishings.

Long ago the wife of the Hub's bouncer was vainly looking for him. Suspecting that he was amusing himself somewhere along Blair Street—Siverton's celebrated Boulevard of Easy Virtue—she exclaimed angrily "If I don't find that sonofabitch soon, there'll be a hot time in the old town tonight!" Her words inspired one of the guests to sit down and write the famous song of the same title. Thus musical history was made in the Hub Saloon. The Grand Imperial also has a lifesized portrait of Lillian Russel at the top of its classic winding staircase. She was one of the Hub's star performers. . . .

Silverton, the "Mining Town that Never Quit" is the terminal of the narrow-guage Silverton-Durango railroad, a great tourist favorite. Towards the north stretches the famous Million Dollar Highway towards Ouray. "The Switzerland of the Rockies," also called "The Opal of the Mountains." Its first building was a saloon "where whisky glasses were used up faster than they could be washed. So, they stopped washing them." This was the haunt of a girl named Charlotte whose obituary became famous:

Charlotte,
Born a virgin, died a harlot.
For 14 years she kept her virginity,
An all-time record for this vicinity.

The saloon, unfortunately, ended up as a courthouse. . . .

The town of Creede, Colorado, is famous as the place where Bob

Ford, "the dirty little coward who shot down Mister Howard, and laid poor Jesse in the grave," got his just deserts. Ford owned and operated the Exchange, a combination saloon and gambling den. One day Ed O'Kelley walked into the place and shot down Bob Ford "in such a way that his gold collar button came out at the back of his neck," thereby avenging his murder of Jesse James. The funeral was marked by a stupendous whiskey-swilling party on boot hill with "dancing on the grave and a great deal of fornication taking place among the headstones."

Creede was a wide-awake town:

It's day all day in the daytime,
And there's no night in Creede.

. . . In Jackson Hole, Wyoming, thirsty pilgrims should not fail to visit the Stagecoach Bar in Wilson. It is neither old, nor historical, nor architecturally remarkable. It is a dingy, red-painted box of a building with a tin roof, but it is very colorful because of the unique characters who make up its clientele, many of them grizzled ex-rodeo champs. The whole place has a very horsey atmosphere and actually stands on an abandoned, weedy rodeo grounds. It is said that some riders performed right inside the bar and that a few of them tried to shoot pool from horseback. One regular likes to eat money for a chaser—nothing less than a ten-spot will satisfy his taste. One lady customer generally does her drinking while fully stretched out on the bar on which she also frequently goes to sleep. To dislodge her, firecrackers are sometimes lit beneath her ample

---

 You Can Also Rub It on Wounds   The world's strongest beer is Thomas Hardy's Ale brewed in July 1968 by the Dorchester Brewery of Dorset, England. It is 10.15 percent alcohol by weight and 12.58 percent by volume.

---

seat. Another client always makes his exit by diving through the window, careless of whether it is open or not. During an earthquake the nearby cabin of an old codger was badly shaken up. He appeared promptly at the saloon in his winter underwear, waving his shotgun at the blamed drunks who tried to push his shack around. The Stage Coach is probably the only bar where a sea lion was nabbed on a drunk and disorderly. The hapless creature, which belonged to a couple who made animal movies, escaped from its pen one dark night. It wandered into the saloon, bellied up to the bar and banged its flippers energetically on the counter as if demanding a drink. Luckily the sheriff was right there, bending an elbow with the boys, and the poor sea lion wound up in the drunk tank. I got the story straight from the owners of the beast which, incidentally, was below the legal drinking age and deserved what it got. . . .

Virginia City, Nevada, home of the fabled Comstock Mine, is a saloon-hunter's paradise, for it is the site of the still operating "One and only *Original* Bucket of Blood Saloon." In front of the Bucket stands an ancient hearse—or gut-wagon. Customers pose for snapshots in the open coffin. Among the customers who cashed in their chips in the Bucket was a fallen angel called Maggie. Her demise is still recalled in a song of some dozen verses:

> *Who shot Maggie in the freckle?*
> *Who shot Maggie in the divide?*
> *Who pierced her billowing bloomers?*
> *And ran away to hide?*

This is the one printable verse. For women's libbers this saloon has interest for having employed the first lady bouncer, Madame Bulldog, who weighed 220 pounds stripped and, according to those who knew her, was that way most of the time. The Bucket's clientele was supposed to be so tough that they disdained to drink anything weaker than undiluted sulphuric acid. . . .

A tour of the alcoholic West leaves one mellow and aglow with the knowledge that enough of the old, well-beloved bucket shops remain to warm the cockles of a drinking man's heart. As the saying goes: "The history of Greece is told in its monuments, the history of the American West in its saloons."

with an honest old friend

by henry carey

(d. 1743)

WITH an honest old friend and a merry old song,
And a flask of old port let me sit the night long,
And laugh at the malice of those who repine
That they must drink porter whilst I can drink wine.

I envy no mortal though ever so great,
Nor scorn I a wretch for his lowly estate;
But what I abhor and esteem as a curse,
Is poorness of spirit, not poorness of purse.

Then dare to be generous, dauntless and gay,
Let us merrily pass life's remainder away;
Upheld by our friends, we our foes may despise,
For the more we are envied, the higher we rise.

"Guess what I made with a little alcohol last night."

Professor Birmingham takes to the rostrum again, and by the time you finish this piece, you'll know the origin of the word gin.

The origin of the word martini, however, is still one of the three great mysteries of our time. The other two, or course, are "Where do the elephants go to die?" and "Why is there a law against taking those little tags off mattresses?"

from martini to vartini

by frederic birmingham

FOR those eternal optimists who by now are suffering from strictures of the inner ear from the repetitious cry—"a dry Martini, *very* dry"—I have good news. The status seekers who have been announcing themselves thus in our favorite spots over the past several seasons will soon be one with the automobile klaxon, the Graham Cracker, and Billy Van's Pine Tree Soap, all of which deserved a kinder fate.

One of the reasons is, of course, due to the inexorable logic of the show-off syndrome—to be different, one must be different. Now that everyone is wearing a suit with a vest and driving a car with an engine originally designed for a sewing machine, there is a grand trend toward velvet smoking jackets and Buicks among the innovators.

Chief casualty in this paradoxical switch, I am happy to say, will be the lads who have brought that noblest of drinks, the Martini, to its present low estate in what may be called its burlesque version—The Naked Martini. No vermouth at all. Just gin on the rocks.

In a more elegant era than our own, the Martini was served with more vermouth in it than in our own day. Straight gin was only encountered in the dreams of charwomen and in the depictions of George Cruikshank and Hogarth. And indeed, why not? Gin itself is a subtle compound of pure grain alcohol, water, and the flavor of juniper berries, cassia bark, coriander seed, angelica root, anise seed, sweet and bitter orange peel, bitter almonds, fennel, orris root, and other inspirational herbs. This permits infinite variation (on the part of the producer), in contrast, say, to vodka, which is straight grain alcohol and has infinite niceties of flavor to explore before you find your favorite brand. But think what the vermouth adds to this

"You mean if I sow liquor and dames, I'll reap liquor and dames?"

already complex flavor; vermouth has a white wine base, boosted with shots of grape brandy, and then made fragrant with varying amounts of leaves of peppermint, plants of yarrow, bark of wormwood, roots of valerian and gentian, buds and fruits of poplar,

---

Dr. Pepper by Any Other Name   The weakest alcoholic liquid ever sold was a sweet ersatz beer that was brewed in Germany in 1918. It had an original gravity of 1,000.96°.

---

cardamon and currant, flower of camomile, lungwort, juniper berries, and other secret ingredients. A naked Martini indeed!—you're missing half the essences of this fragrant world!

Winston Churchill may well have started the move away from the "yellow Martini," with plenty of vermouth, favored by cosmopolitan gentlemen for generations, simply by mixing his Martinis with, as he said, gin and a glance at the vermouth bottle. But cutting out the vermouth will not turn the little lambs of our poshest drinking places into roaring British lions, hard as they may berate the bored bartenders with their cries for ever drier Martinis.

No, what they need is a swing to the left, a shift into another drink or another way of preparing a Martini, which the majority doesn't seem to know yet. And fortunately this is precisely what's happening. There are a number of ways in which you may embarrass your companions by superior savvy in the art of Martini mixing, and soon these will be all the rage.

The first is the Zubrovka Vartini. Zubrovka, in brief, is a Czech vodka, colored slightly yellow and flavored somewhat by a stalk of grain which sits right in the bottle.

The Vartini is made with a proportion of two parts gin, two parts vodka, and one part vermouth. The flavor is light, the wallop strong.

But the very latest is The Pink Martini. This is made, in the usual proportions, of gin and Campari. The latter is an Italian vermouth, but unlike the familiar sweet variety, it has a very strong and quite bitter flavor. After you've acquired the taste, you'll enjoy it as an aperitif, in a tall glass filled with ice, and enlivened with a twist of lemon and a splash of sparkling water.

Of course, to really be in the know, sophisticated drinkers follow the lead of the French and are given to the Vermouth Cassis. This can be an even-up mixture of dry and sweet vermouth, iced, or dry vermouth mixed with Creme de Cassis and touched with soda water. The British "Gin & It," after all, is merely gin and Italian vermouth, mixed half and half with a splash of soda and *not* iced, if you please, old boy.

If you'd like to make a gesture and impress your companion, then, don't bellow for something drier. Suggest to the bartender that he pour the vermouth first, over the ice, and then pour it off before adding the gin. That's a nice strong, but civilized Martini. Or perhaps suggest that he rinse the glasses with Pernod before pouring the Martinis. And a knowledgeable drinker never has his Martini with the lemon twist *in* it! The rind is given a brisk twist to drop the oils on the surface of the Martini, touched to the rim of the glass, and then properly discarded. Its contribution is never overwhelming this way, and it doesn't displace anything preciously liquid.

"But he's buying."

Where did gin get its name? From Ginievre or Geneva, where the liquor was first made. There are two major types of gin, Geneva and London. Geneva gin is often called schnapps, although the term is also applied to whiskies in the Low Countries. The thing to remember about Geneva gin is that it has a powerful, acrid flavor, the result of putting all its ingredients together and then distilling it out of the complete mash, like whiskey. It is also called Dutch or Holland or Schiedam gin, but you're not apt to regard it favorably unless you have lumbago, in which case the schnapps puts up a real fight against the pains.

London gin is the kind we drink, the difference in manufacture being that the berries and the whatnots are put in the still with raw alcohol (not with the grains, as in Holland) and the alcohol picks up the flavors as it is re-distilled.

We drink dry gin, but there is also a sweet gin, known as Old Tom, which is hardly ever found here. It is simply dry gin with sugar added. It was the original ingredient of the Tom Collins, but the custom has died off since Old Tom is so scarce.

What is sloe gin? It isn't gin at all: it's sloeberry liqueur.

And where did the Martini get its name? No one knows. The Martini & Rossi people (who are not aware of this article, by the way) genially acknowledge that it wasn't named after them, although they wish it had been. We can only conjecture that some humble genius behind a bar once received the inspiration to mix gin and vermouth and thus immortalized himself.

It is a name not unmusical. It is a name nicely attuned to the whisper of winds blowing over snow and through the junipers, and the redolence of gardens where grow those miraculous herbs. It is a name that combines harmoniously with the tinkle of ice, and a fine glass held lightly in the hand. And lastly, it is not a status symbol, but a blessing—and should be kept that way.

Just because you know that Washington crossed the Delaware and Columbus was Jewish, you probably think you're a history whiz. But do you know what Moses called a cool one? Bill Iversen can tell you, as well as the name of the ancient folk epic of the Finns, information so special that even most of the Finns don't know—or care.

keg o' my heart

by william iversen

BEER is the original and authentic booze. The name *boozah* was given to the merry malt beverage by the ancient Egyptians over 5000 years ago, when a superior brand of suds was brewed in the delta city of Busiris. Tomb paintings, papyri and hieroglyphs all attest to the fact that beer was the Egyptian national drink. Two gallons was the minimum daily quota quaffed by even the lowliest sons and daughters of the Nile, and temple priests made light work of religiously chugalugging the daily beer offerings made to Egyptian deities by Pharaoh and his followers. On a typical feast day in old Memphis, over 900 jugs of beer were offered to the god Ptah alone, and Ramsees III is credited with picking up the tab for 466,303 jugs used to slake the eternal thirst of the holy guzzlers.

Brewed of barley, wheat or millet (a kind of seed now sold as a treat for parakeets), Egyptian beer was often spiced or perfumed, and always consumed in quantity. In one tomb painting a lightly clad tavern maid is seen exhorting the customer to drain his crock for a foamy refill. "Drink unto rapture," she coaxes in come-hither hieroglyphs. "Let it be a good day. Listen to the conversation of thy companions and enjoy thyself." When after-dinner beer was served in the palaces of the wealthy, servants would exhibit a wooden "skeleton at the feast" to all the guests, urging them to "Drink and be merry; for when you die, such will you be."

Since the demand was great, and the beer highly perishable, brewing was an everyday task, and was considered a kitchen art, like baking. "Beer is liquid bread," the chemist Liebig observed in the 19th Century, and the Egyptian housewife whipped up a batch of homebrew along with her loaves and spice cakes. In the brewing kitchens of the nobility, professional brewers made beer for households numbering in the hundreds, and a list of such brewers' names in the Petrie Papyri has left scholars puzzling over a mystery greater than the riddle of the Sphinx. According to an Egyptologist named Mahaffy, who made a study of the scrolls, one strangely un-Egyptian name keeps reappearing: "It is the name SMITH, undeniably written this way in Greek letters."

Who Smith was, or where he came from, no one knows. Despite the Greek lettering of his name, it is not considered likely that this brewer to the Third Ptolemy was of Hellenic origin, since the Greeks were a winebibbing people and had even less understanding of cereal beverages than the grape-oriented Romans and Hebrews. It should be noted, though, that a former Cairo brewery official, named James Death, once wrote a book that attempted to prove that the "leavened bread" of the Bible was, in reality, Jewish beer, which the Israelites learned to make during their captivity in Egypt.

Actually, the primitive brewing process was so simple that anyone could have learned it at a glance. In the case of the Egyptians, grain was moistened with water and allowed to stand until it began to germinate, at which time it was dried and ground into a coarse malt. The malt was then steeped in a vat of hot water and yeasted with

Standing at a bar one day, W. C. Fields ordered Scotch and a water chaser. He put his fingers into the water, wiped them on a napkin, and then said to the bartender, "Make it another one and another chaser. I don't like to bathe in the same water twice."

sour bread and dough. When fermentation had taken place, and the yeast had converted the grain sugars into alcohol, the foaming beer was then strained off into jugs.

By this same basic process, beer had been brewed since the dawn of thirst by people from the southern tip of Africa to the Arctic Circle. Yeasts and cereals varied according to climate, however. In Africa the fermentation of native millet beers is still induced by means of milkweed and fermented roots. In the *Kalevala*, the ancient folk epic of the Finns, the saga of the search for yeast is told in the same iambic pentameter as Longfellow's *Hiawatha*:

> *What will bring the effervescence,*
> *Who will add the needed factor,*
> *That the beer may foam and sparkle,*
> *May ferment and be delightful?*

"You're sick!"

With a mythological assist from Kapo, "snowy virgin of the Northland," the old brewess tries adding ripe pine cones and foam from the mouths of angry bears, with no success. Finally, honey is tried, and the beer begins to ferment, "Foaming higher, higher, higher . . . /Overflowing all the caldrons." The news travels fast:

> Scarce a moment had passed over,
> Ere the heroes came in numbers,
> To the foaming beer of Northland,
> Rushed to drink the sparkling liquor . . .
> Said to make the feeble hardy,
> Famed to dry the tears of women,
> Famed to cheer the broken-hearted,
> Make the aged young and supple,
> Make the timid brave and mighty,
> Make the brave men even braver,
> Fill the heart with joy and gladness,
> Fill the mind with wisdom sayings,
> Fill the tongue with ancient legends . . .

Among the most ancient of Norse legends was the story of Valhalla, where Odin's armored maidens, the Valkyries, greeted slain heroes with brimming ale horns, and heaven consisted of an eternity of booze on the house. Since distinct differences between ale and beer had yet to evolve, malt brew was called both *öl* and *biorr*.

Told by a young doctor that he would be dead in six months if he didn't stop drinking, W. C. Fields replied, "Why, that's exactly what a German medico in Baden-Baden told me twenty-eight years ago. I'm glad to see that you doctors agree on something."

Common to all Northern languages was some form of *biorr*, which etymologists have traced to *beo*, a word which the Old Germans used for "barley" and Anglo-Saxons applied to the yeast-yielding honeybee. From this double-barreled source we got *beor*, *biorr*, *bere* and, eventually, *beer*.

Differences in nomenclature aside, the heroes of the North were never at a loss for an excuse to pass around horns of the wet and foamy. Ale was drunk in thanksgiving for the harvest and in penance for one's sins, to celebrate births and marriages, and to make the mourners merry at wakes. Long before the beery reigns of Harald Bluetooth and Gorm the Old, ancient Danes gave "ales" in the same way that 19th Century English ladies gave "teas." Every sort of meeting, secular or religious, was called an "ale," for the same refreshment was served at all, whether held in a sacred grove, a family hall or the council room of a king. Saxon chiefs would never sit to decide an important matter without first whetting their wisdom with large *humpen* of brew, and Norwegians held that business transacted at an ale drinking was as legal and binding as any performed in a court of law.

From the beginning of the Christian era, beer became as closely associated with the northern Church as it had previously been with pagan religion. Saint Brigit, the Fifth Century abbess of Kildare, is still remembered for having miraculously transformed a tub of bath water into most excellent beer to assuage the thirst of lepers. The good saint held Irish brew in such high esteem that she was moved to declare, "I would like to have a great lake of beer for Christ the King. I would like to be watching the Heavenly Family drinking it down through all eternity."

Throughout the Middle Ages, beer was served at breakfast, dinner and supper, and the per-capita consumption is estimated to have been in the vicinity of eight quarts a day. Brewing for a large feudal estate was, therefore, a major operation. In Wales, where beer was called *cwrw* by drunk and sober alike, the royal brewer ranked above the court physician, and it was the king's privilege to sample privately every new cask of ale. It was further ordained that the high-ranking steward should receive "as much of every cask of plain ale as he can reach with his middle finger dipped into it, and as much of every cask of ale with spiceries as he can reach with the second joint of his middle finger."

The steward's finger was by no means the first to be put into the beer. The age-old custom of dipping a digit into a vat to determine

---

Someone once said to W. C. Fields, "Mr. Fields, what would your father have said if he had known that you drank two quarts of whiskey a day?"
    "He would have called me a sissy," Fields replied.

---

the temperature of a malt mixture was already known as "the rule of thumb," for brewing remained an instinctive art practiced mainly by women in their kitchens. A girl learned to make ale at her mother's knee, and counted the ability among her beau-catching accomplishments. When she married, the bride and her mother brewed a big batch, and gave a "bride ale" feast to which friends and neighbors brought gifts to start the young couple in housekeeping—and in this we have the beery beginnings of all bridal parties.

Among the feasts and ceremonies retained from pagan days were the old religious "ales," which were adapted to the celebration of Christian festivals in the Middle Ages. There were Whitsun ales,

---

This is what I now propose:
In a tavern I shall die
With a glass up to my nose
And God's angels standing by
That they may indeed declare
As I take my final tot
May God receive with loving care
Such a decent drunken sot.

—FOURTEENTH-CENTURY LATIN TOAST

Easter ales, tithe ales, and ales in memory of saints and the dear departed. On the eve of a saint's day, people would gather in the churchyard, as they had formerly gathered in sacred groves, with beer and food to see them through the long night's vigil. As a Tenth Century manuscript describes it, they came "with candelys burnyng, and would wake, and come toward night to the church of their devocian." And "afterwards the pepul fell to letcherie, and songs, and daunses, with harping and piping, and also to glotony and sinne."

Against all such unbuttoned "ales" and dubious devotions, the higher clergy of Britain, Germany, Scandinavia and Flanders issued repeated warnings. But nowhere was better beer brewed than in the convents and monasteries, where brotherly brewers and cloistered brewesses worked to perfect their beers with a precision of method unknown to any other branch of medieval science. At a time when the taste and quality of home-brewed beers varied from house to house, and from one batch to the next, monastic brewers were striving to standardize their product by means of grain selection, temperature control, and the exact measurement of malt and "spicer-ies." The familiar XXX symbol for strong booze began with the monastic grading of beers into one-, two- and three-X qualities, and the first significant step toward the development of modern beer is believed to have been made in a convent kitchen with the experimental use of hops.

Though hops are mentioned in the Finnish *Kalevala*, and Belgians credit the invention of hopped beer to a 13th Century Flemish king,

Gambrinus, the first reliable reference to the use of hops in beer occurs in the *Physica Sacra* of Saint Hildegard. Speaking *De Hoppho*, the 12th Century German saint wrote that while its bitterness gave beer "a longer durability," the hop "creates in man a sad mood" and "affects his bowels unpleasantly by reason of its heating properties." In the third volume of the same work, she therefore advises, "If thou desirest to make a beer from oats and hops, boil it also with the addition of *Gruz* and several ash leaves, as such a beer purges the stomach of the drinker and eases his chest."

To this day, the exact nature of *Gruz* is unknown, though brewers and scholars generally agree that it doesn't sound like anything the modern drinker would like to have in his beer. The theory is that *Gruz* was a seasoning compounded of plants and herbs, such as sweet gale, wild rosemary, yarrow, juniper, bog myrtle, broom tops, alehoof and moth-kraut. Whatever its ingredients, it is known that the Archbishop of Cologne had a monopoly on its manufacture in 1381 and that German *Gruz*, or *Grut*, beers were brewed and sold for export in Hamburg, Bremen, Lübeck, Münster and Einbeck during the 11th Century.

The fame of Einbeck's wheat-and-barley beer was such that brewers in other towns began to imitate the summer brew, which was called *Ainpock*, or *Einbock.* In time, the name was shortened to *Bock*—the German word for "goat"—and all reference to Einbeck was lost when the head of a bucking goat was adopted as its universal trademark.

Among the most popular beers of the Middle Ages were the light, hopped wheat beers of Bohemia, which were often favored over the native product by drinkers in the leading beer towns of Germany. The importation and enormous sale of Bohemian beer by the cathedral chapter of Breslau created such economic havoc with the town's brewing industry that brewers and councilmen joined forces to make the trade illegal, thus touching off the *Pfaffenkrieg*, or "Parsons' War," of 1380. Denied their traditional right to sell beer of any origin, the clergy closed the churches and refused to perform all sacraments.

In the equally memorable year 1492, when Columbus set sail to discover the West Indies and a hitherto unknown malady called syphilis, a sensible stay-at-home German brewer of Braunschweig, named Christian Mumme, is said to have concocted a thickish, hopped barley beer, which later became a favorite in London. Most Englishmen found the hopped German beers too bitter for their taste, however, and preferred the more saccharine English ales.

Because of the spicy sweetness of their ale, the English tradition-

"'Sleep tight,' yourself."

ally drank it with festive cakes and fruit, in consequence of which custom King John was reported to have died, not of his enemies' poison, but of a "surfeit of new ale and peaches"—a combination that impresses one present-day American beer drinker as being pretty much the same thing. In an effort to explain the early English distinction between ale and beer, a 19th Century authority theorized that ale was "brewed from malt to be drunk fresh," while beer was "brewed from malt and hops, intended to keep." But the same writer found that distinctions were "different in different parts of the country," even in his own day, and failed to take into account that the word "bere," or "beer," had been in use long before the English fancied the flavor of hops. The most likely explanation is that the terms were used almost interchangeably, since British brews differed widely in taste and strength, and were known by a variety of local names as well.

One reason for the profusion of names and types is that most English householders did their own brewing, or patronized a breed of boozy brewesses, called "alewives," whose recipes were highly individualistic. Recalling the broom-top flavoring used in German *Gruz*, it is significant that the original English alehouse sign was a broom hung outside an alewife's door to inform the thirsty traveler that home-brewed ale was for sale within. This tradition of female "brewsters" carried over into the 15th and 16th Centures, when women not only brewed for London taverns, but frequently ran them.

Insofar as the modern student can ascertain, the brew and services of some lady innkeepers left much to be desired, however. As early as 1464, the male members of the first professional Brewers' Company petitioned the Lord Mayor of London for more rigid regulations against unscrupulous brewesses who made "their bere of unseasonable malt, the which is of little price and unholsome for mannes body." A statute of Henry VIII forbade brewers to use hops and "brimstone." A more liberal attitude toward hops was displayed by Henry's son, Edward VI, however, and the controversial vine grew in English esteem over the following century, eventually winning the scientific approval of herbalist Nicholas Culpepper. Hops, Culpepper held, "easeth the headache that comes of heat" and "killeth the worms in the body."

If Culpepper was correct, the Elizabethans must have been remarkably free from all possible obstructions. The Queen and her maids of honor began each day with pieces of toast floating in quarts of warm ale. Mary, Queen of Scots, who was weaned on beer as a tot, expressed anxiety over the supply as soon as she was imprisoned in Tutbury Castle, and sent her secretary to inquire, "At what place near Tutbury may beer be provided for Her Majesty?"

"Beer may be had at Burton," the secretary was told, and, according to all accounts, Burton brew was indeed fit for a queen. Its chief Elizabethan competitors were "March beer," which required an aging of two years, and the ale that was sold at the sign of the Dagger, in Holborn.

"We must have March bere, dooble, dooble beer, and Dagger ale," Thomas Dekker declared, and brew of all types and grades was joyously guzzled in Maytime, haytime, or on any old day of the week. "Cakes and ale" were synonymous with merrymaking. "Beer and skittles" (a kind of ninepins) came to mean any sort of fun and games.

He that drinks strong beer and goes to bed mellow,
Lives as he ought to live, and dies a hearty fellow.

Such was the credo of John Fletcher, the Mermaid tavern wit, who lived to drink the healths of Elizabeth, James and Charles I. Following the execution of Charles by Cromwell's Puritans, beer quickly lost status among the royalists—not because the Puritans were opposed to malt liquor, but because they approved of it. With the overthrow of the monarchy by Cromwell, royalists drank foreign wines and scorned to visit alehouses. Came the Restoration, and the monarchy was re-established, but English brew never quite re-

The public house is a first-aid post in which human beings receive treatment for injuries sustained in the battle with life.

—ANON.

covered from the effects of royalist ridicule. Beer and ale had already disappeared from the tables of the fashionable, who now delighted in a new dinner beverage—hot tea, sipped from saucers. When the Great Turk Coffeehouse opened, in 1662, even breakfast ale was threatened by creeping coffee addiction, and malt brew of any sort became a lower-class drink.

But not for long. Twenty-seven years later, William of Orange arrived from the Netherlands with a retinue of Dutch courtiers and a regal supply of brandy and Holland gin. Though the Irish and Scots had been distilling whiskey for centuries, English fondness for strong liquor dates only from 1690, when William's government passed "An Act for the Encouraging of the Distillation of Brandy and Spirits." Stills sprang up everywhere, and within four years the annual production of English gin rose to a million gallons. Because of its potency and cheapness, gin became the favorite tipple of the common man.

Wealthier and more discriminating citizens savored brandy, and cultivated a connoisseurship of Continental wines. The classless simplicity of all-purpose table beer was lost in the ritualized consumption of correct vintages. Where toast, fruit, raw eggs and other foods were formerly added to ale, wine and brandy were now added to foods. English brewing degenerated.

In Germany, Scandinavia and the Low Countries, the story was much the same. With the advent of distilled schnapps, the bravura beer drinkers of Brueghel and Rubens became moody dram nippers, and brewing went into decline. By 1728, the quality of German beer sank so low that Frederick William I denounced the brewers of Potsdam, declaring that the King of Prussia had "had their watery, sour unwholesome slops going by the name of beer in his eye about long enough." Threatening to appoint a whole new set of brewers, he ordered that his son, Frederick, be instructed in the art of brewing in preparation for the day when he would succeed to the throne. By the time young Frederick became "the Great," however, the Prussian passion for imported coffee was draining the royal treasury. "It is disgusting to notice the increase in the quantity of coffee used by my subjects," he wrote in 1777. "If possible this must be prevented. My people must drink beer. His Majesty was brought up on beer and so were his ancestors, and his officers and soldiers."

Among Frederick's beer-fed army brass was a little-known drill instructor named Steuben, who assumed the title of Baron in order to hoax his way into the service of the American Continental Army, where his genius won the respect of another beer-drinking military man—General George Washington, who made his own home-brew, in keeping with a Colonial tradition which started with the Pilgrim Fathers. The Mayflower, as one shipboard journal noted, was actually on its way to Virginia, and landed passengers at Plymouth Rock only because "we could not now take time for further search or consideration: our victuals being spent, especially our beere. . . ." Once settled ashore, the parched Puritans wasted no time in putting their crocks and kettles to work. The first commercial brewery in Massachusetts opened in 1634, and was soon followed by others in Connecticut and Rhode Island. In New Amsterdam, the methodical Dutch started a full-scale beer works north of Wall Street.

According to William Penn, the quaffing Quaker, who made and sold beer at Pennsbury, Pennsylvania, early settlers in the state improvised homebrew "of Molasses, which well-boyld, with Sassafras or Pine infused into it, makes a very tolerable drink." In the Southern colonies, less tolerable beer was brewed of dried cornstalks, persimmons, potatoes and Jerusalem artichokes.

By 1710, the cheapness of West Indian rum, and the quick Yankee grasp of the principles of distilling, had made beer brewing a

---

 Safe at Home   When a manager told baseball player Dusty Rhodes to cut his boozing in half, Rhodes replied he already had done so. "I quit drinking chasers," he said.

---

marginal occupation. Since stills were tax-free and easy to build, farmers converted their grain into easily shipped kegs of whiskey for sale to taverns and grocery stores.

Back in England, meanwhile, a 20-shilling-per-gallon tax on spirits had raised prices to a level where the workingman was forced to drink malt brew in defense of his pocketbook. Some drank beer and some drank ale, while some favored a combination of the two known as "half-and-half." Others inclined to a three-way mixture of strong beer, light beer and ale, which kept publicans hopping from one keg to another filling mugs, until a brewer named Harwood hit upon the idea of packaging the three brews in one keg. Harwood called the mixture "entire," but it quickly became known as "porter"—presumably because of its popularity among thirsty London porters. In less plebeian taprooms, gentlemen often requested a stronger, higher-priced ale called "stout," and kept count of their pints and quarts by chalking the score on the table—thus "minding their Ps and Qs."

When America's score with the British was settled, and Hessian mercenaries had gone home to Germany to seek solace in steins of Frederick the Great's patriotically improved beers, the victorious Yankees went back to hitting the jug in jubilation. Rum sotting and whiskey snorting threatened to become the American way of life, and the Massachusetts legislature sat in 1789 to find a way of limiting drunkenness without curtailing independence. The result was "An Act to Encourage the Manufacture of Strong Beer, Ale and Other Malt Liquors," in which commercial brewers were exempted from all taxes for a period of five years. But tax-free breweries still couldn't compete with tax-free stills—of which there were 5000 in Pennsylvania alone.

Much of the American aversion to malt brew may be attributed to the fact that early 19th Century beers were flat and dull. They tasted moral, and bore little resemblance to our lively latter-day product. Modern beer, or "lager," was the inspired creation of some unknown German brewer or brewers, and involved the use of a yeast that sank into the brewing mixture, instead of floating on top, thereby causing fermentation to work up from the bottom. Additional liveliness was induced by krausening, or carbonation.

Lager was first brewed in the United States by a German brewer named Wagner, who made the first batch in a shanty on the outskirts of Philadelphia in 1842. Its success among the German-Americans of Philadelphia was instantaneous, and with the growing influx of German immigrants, other brewers began making lager to supply the ever-increasing number of beer saloons in the German neighborhoods of Eastern cities.

Among native Americans, however, drunkenness remained a national problem in the years preceding the Civil War. Seventeen states had experimented with prohibition by 1855, but Yankees and Rebels continued to enjoy the strong comfort of whiskey and moonshine all during the Great Conflict. The stillness at Appomattox was followed by renewed keg thumping on behalf of beer, whose temperance virtues were now underscored by the solid citizenship of the industrious German-Americans of the North.

An 1866 report of the U.S. Department of Agriculture found that "a moderate use of beer will aid digestion, quicken the powers of life, and give elasticity to the body and mind." More appealing to the average American was the lively taste of lager, and a growing appreciation of the brew made beer the basic beverage in New York's new "concert saloons" and German-type beer gardens. A fastidious French tourist, named Longchamp, tells of an 1867 visit to one of these pretzel palaces, which he found "handsomely fitted up, and crowded with visitors—a number of what they call 'pretty waiter girls' flitting about among the customers, and laughing and loudly talking with them. A piano player, wildly thumping and banging on a cracked and hideously wired instrument, the rattling of glasses, and moving of chairs and tables—all contributed to bewilder and madden me . . ."

The sight and sound of so much happy guzzling bewildered and maddened many former advocates of beer temperance, too. The dutiful sipping of warm, flat prelager brews as a substitute for "ardent spirits" was to be admired, but the genuine enjoyment of cool, refreshing lager in saloons where "pretty waiter girls" served whiskey, brandy and rum, as well—that, of course, was something

"I think Miss Meadows has had a little too much to drink."

to be deplored. By 1880, annual lager production was up to 13,500,000 barrels, and in the next decade it doubled. Beer had become the American fun drink, and if the Nineties were gay, lager could justly claim a good part of the credit. The large foaming mug and the small five-cent price still symbolize "the good old days," and the corner saloon with its sleek mahogany bar, brass rail, swinging doors, free lunch and genuine handpainted study of a romantic nude, epitomizes the happy past for all who take their nostalgia in gulps.

The *Gemütlichkeit* that beer promoted on the working-class level was counterbalanced by the urban elegance described by O. Henry in his purple-tinted snapshot of *A Cosmopolite in a Café*: "I invoke your consideration of the scene—the marble-topped tables, the range of leather-upholstered wall seats, the gay company, the ladies dressed in demistate toilets, speaking in an exquisite visible chorus of taste . . ."

From the melting-pot neighborhoods to the haunts of the upper strata, the revolution that lager had worked upon American social life was all but complete, and tastes were beginning to reflect a new sophistication. Pasteurization, which Pasteur developed from his studies in beer fermentation, now made it possible to enjoy bottled beers that were free of deterioration caused by active microorganisms. German beers were imported to New York, Milwaukee beers were available in Alabama.

But lager was doomed by its very success. Militant prohibitionists no longer discriminated between beer and ardent spirits. They were antisaloon, and since beer had built the American saloon, they were

---

*Malt does more than Milton can
To reconcile God's ways to man.*

—A.E. HOUSMAN (1859–1936)

---

out to ban beer. Through the agitation of feminist reformers, Prohibition was emotionally linked with the fight for woman suffrage. The clergy and large corporations joined the crusade to stamp out "the curse of drink," and when the Kaiser's army overran "little Belgium," in 1914, American indignation was directed against beer as a German beverage. No one thought to point out that the Belgian victims were themselves the world's leading beer drinkers, with a per-capita capacity almost twice that of the German invaders, and by the time America entered the War, beer had few public defenders.

The Volstead Prohibition Act of 1919 gave only token approval to the former temperance drink by allowing the manufacture and sale of a beer that would contain no more than one half of one percent alcohol.

The new low-key lager was dubbed "near-beer," and Luke McLuke of *The Cincinnati Enquirer* sadly commented that the man who first called it that was a mighty poor judge of distance. Many brewers went out of business rather than produce such wishy-washy suds. Some kept their plants intact and sat back to await the failure of the Noble Experiment, while others brewed near-beer as an adjunct to making the soda and ginger ale Americans now needed to dilute raw bootleg hooch. Of all outlawed liquids, lager was the most difficult to bootleg. Since beer could not be brewed profitably in bathtubs, bootleggers would purchase breweries through dummy corporations and produce enough de-alcoholized beer to satisfy appearances, while vats of full-strength lager were piped off into a nearby garage for delivery to speak-easies. Others supplied their near-beer customers with a supplement of alcohol, which could be added or "needled" into a glass or keg of legal brew to bring it up to full strength.

As an alternative to drinking the questionable fluids at high prices, economy-minded quaffers made their own home-brew from ingredients sold in malt-and-hops shops, but, for all its purity, homebrew was usually inferior in foam and flavor to the worst in the bootlegger's stable. Small wonder, then, at the rejoicing on April 7, 1933, when a New Deal law legalized the sale of 3.2 lager, which was only .5 short of pre-Prohibition strength. In cities and towns from coast to coast, crowds gathered in a New Year's Eve mood to celebrate the end of the 14-year dry spell. In Times Square, a mock funeral for near-beer was held amidst shouted choruses of *Happy Days Are Here Again.* A Milwaukee brewery threw open its doors to cheering celebrants and doled out free beer to all who brought a container. In the 20 states where the law was immediately effective, lager was sold in restaurants, lunchrooms, hastily equipped taverns and drugstore soda fountains. A million barrels were joyously guzzled in the first 24 hours, and breweries ran dry.

The first canned beers hit the market in the mid-Thirties and, by 1939, beer-can punchers shared the homey clutter of kitchen drawers. In neighborhood beer stubes a brassy-voiced girl trio, called the Andrews Sisters, was rattling glasses with the *Beer Barrel Polka,* a raucous recording that became the American beer drinker's national anthem. Sentimental customers fed a few nickels into the slot and sipped their brew to the strains of *Our Love* and *I Didn't Know What*

Time It Was. Actually, it was later than most Americans imagined. In the previous September, England's Prime Minister Chamberlain had flown to Munich, beer capital of Bavaria, to play a losing hand for peace with Nazi Chancellor Adolf Hitler.

Once again the beer-drinking Belgians were overrun, but Americans knew better than to hold beer responsible for German aggression. British pub patrons were braving out the blitz with the help of an occasional pint, and Yanks in uniform drank their beer to the tune of *Praise the Lord and Pass the Ammunition, When the Lights Go On Again* and the *Victory Polka.* GIs stationed in England grew familiar with aromatic British ale, beer and stout served at the warmish temperatures natural to a nation reluctant to accept central heating. In occupied Germany and Austria they met with a wide variety of lagers, ranging from light, dry Pilsner types that resembled the better American brews, to the darker, sweeter beers characteristic of Bavaria. Color, they soon found, had little to do with a beer's strength or body. A bottle of pale Danish beer purchased in post-War Paris might have a fuller body and higher alcoholic content than a dark table beer which Belgians drank in place of water.

For the most part, however, the GI preference was for the familiar American beers, which varied somewhat in flavor from brand to brand, but were similarly light, dry, medium-strong and refreshingly effervescent. From repeal to the present day, beers of this type have been favored by the majority of Americans in all sections of the country. Minority drinkers, who appreciate differences, are more than likely to hit upon a brew to their liking among such relatively offbeat American types as Prior's Double Dark, Pittsburgh's Iron City Beer, and robust Rainier Old Stock Ale and Danish-yeasted Olympia Beer of the Pacific Northwest, and such premium draught beers as Michelob or Pabst Andeker.

Fortunately, beer has no sacrosanct vintages. In selecting a brew, there's nothing to do but quaff and compare, and the urban beer buff is by no means confined to domestic brands. Over the past ten years or so, American travel abroad has created an increasing demand for foreign beers, and a bewitching bevy of bottled imports share supermarket shelves with canned *Geschlürf* from Milwaukee and "merry-go-down" from Detroit. Pushing a cart through the beer section of a well-stocked metropolitan market, the serious sudsman can fill his basket with a library of famous brews: Amstel and Heineken's from Holland; Carlsberg and Tuborg from Denmark; Löwenbräu and Würzburger from Germany; Carta Blanca from Mexico; Kirin from Japan; Guinness Stout and Harp Lager from Ireland; Bass and Whitbread English Ales; and an occasional sampling of Czechoslovakian Pilsner Urquell. The list is far from complete, and new labels keep turning up to pique the palate.

The greatest single influence on American beer-drinking habits in the past 15 years has been television, which has sharply reduced over-the-bar sales of draught beer, and sent home consumption of packaged beers soaring. In bottles, cans and on draught, American beer consumption has doubled since repeal, with an estimated 15.8 per-capita gallons guzzled in 1964. This was still only about half the

---

*The troubles of our proud and angry dust
Are from eternity, and shall not fail.
Bear them we can, and if we must
Shoulder the sky, my lad, and drink your ale.*

—A.E. HOUSMAN (1859–1936)

---

amount consumed in Belgium in 1963, when the world's champion beer drinkers burped in at 30.6 gallons to beat West Germany's 30.0 by a foam fleck.

If America was lagging behind in the chugalug league, its scientists were making major brew break-throughs. A few years ago the *New York Herald Tribune* heralded the discovery of "A New Drug Found in Beer Said to Clear Mental Illness." The drug, called glutathione, is "made up of three amino acids, the basic chemicals of all protein-life substances," and is therefore essential to man's very existence. In a paper delivered before the Academy of Psychosomatic Medicine, Dr. Mark Altschule of Harvard reported that experimental doses of glutathione were given to disturbed patients, "and removed their excessive mental aberrations for a month." The only drawback to its widespread use is the difficulty of extracting glutathione from whole beer, which puts the cost of a single treatment at "about $1000."

The human digestive tract can do the same extracting job for free, of course. With a $1000 beer budget, it would seem that the normally distressed drinker could enjoy the benefits of therapy for a considerable period of time, while absorbing additional protection against an embolism in old age, by virtue of another element in beer which British researchers find "decreases the rapidity of blood clotting." But science in the Age of Anxiety only confirms the folk wisdom of the Age of Heroes, when rugged warriors of the Northland "Rushed to drink the sparkling liquor . . . / Said to make the feeble hardy . . . / Famed to cheer the broken-hearted . . . / Fill the heart with joy and gladness. . . ." Hops, as old Culpepper discovered, "easeth the headache that comes of heat" and should be used to "cleanse the reins of gravel." As the poet A. E. Housman has pointed out, ". . . malt does more than Milton can/To justify God's ways to man." There's peace of mind in Pilsner, and lager is the liquid staff of life.

Let's drink to that, shall we? Here's to your very good health!

Have you often wondered if white wine is correct with chow mein or if a hero sandwich demands a Burgundy? Well, Kingsley Amis here describes some matchups for you that will bring benedictions from the Lucullan Society.

what to drink
with what

by kingsley amis

What	What to drink with it
Simply-flavoured dishes, hot or cold; mild cheeses of the English variety	Inexpensive clarets like Côtes de Bourg, Côtes de Blaye, Côtes de Fronsac
Beef, lamb, pork, game, poultry, any full-blooded stuff; stronger cheeses, pâté, stews	Givry, Fixin, Dôle, Monthélie, Old Algerian, Mercurey, Morgon, Moulin-à-Vent, Cornas, Lirac, Gigondas, Châteauneuf du Pape, Hermitage, Côte Rôtie, Crozes-Hermitage, St Joseph
Eggs and bacon, eggs and chips, baked beans and sausages	Any of the above, also beer, cider, Guinness, Scotch and water without ice (first-rate)
Hot and cold meats, picnic meals, or nothing at all	Any of the wines listed as going with beef, lamb, pork, etc., plus beaujolais, Beaujolais Villages, Fleurie, Brouilly, Chiroubles
Soups	Sherry, madeira if you're feeling fancy, or the end of your apéritif provided it doesn't contain hard liquor

Oysters	Chablis, Muscadet, Guinness, Black Velvet
Fish and chips	Guinness
Curry	Beer, cider, or try a tough red chianti
Cold dishes, fish, shellfish, salads, picnics	Puligny Montrachet, Meursault, Alsace Riesling or Sylvaner, Tokay d'Alsace, Tavel Rosé (if you must), Sancerre, Pouilly Fumé, Pouilly Fuissé, a non-pricey hock or moselle
Shellfish, jellied eels, cold meats	Gewurtztraminer, Traminer
Vichyssoise, melon, before lunch	Muscat d'Alsace, Piesporter, Zeltinger
Salads, shellfish, cold buffet	Beaujolais Rosé chilled
Hot dishes not heavily spiced	Beaujolais Rosé at room temperature
Desserts, fresh fruit, especially peaches	Quarts de Chaumes, Châteaux Rieusses and Climens, Sauternes, Barsac
Fondue	Neuchâtel will help you to force it down
Anything, everything or nothing	Champagne N.V.

fill the goblet again

by lord byron

(1788–1824)

FILL the goblet again! for I never before
Felt the glow that now gladdens my heart to its core;
Let us drink!—who would not?—since through life's varied
    round
In the goblet alone no deception is found.

I have tried in its turn all that life can supply;
I have basked in the beam of a dark rolling eye;
I have loved!—who has not?—but what heart can declare,
That pleasure existed whilst passion was there?

In the bright days of youth, when the heart's in its spring,
And dream that affection can never take wing,
I had friends!—who has not?—but what tongue will avow,
That friends, rosy wine, are so faithful as thou?

The heart of a mistress some boy may estrange;
Friendship shifts with the sunbeam—thou never canst
    change,
Thou grow'st old!—who does not?—but on earth what
    appears,
Whose virtues, like thine, still increase with its years?

Yet if blest to the utmost that love can bestow,
Should a rival bow down to our idol below,
We are jealous—who's not?—thou hast no such alloy;
For the more that enjoy thee, the more they enjoy.